STRATEGIES THAT MAKE LEARNING FUN!

ISBN 1-57035-915-6

Copy editing by Karen Butler
Text layout and design by Christine Petersen
Cover design by Sue Campbell

07 06   6 5 4 3 2

Printed in the United States of America

Published and Distributed by

SOPRIS
WEST
EDUCATIONAL SERVICES

4093 Specialty Place • Longmont, Colorado 80504
(303) 651-2829
www.sopriswest.com

211LEARN/9-03/VER

ACKNOWLEDGMENTS

The continuing professional support of Stu Horsfall, Steve Mitchell, Ray Beck, Steve Kukic, and Rebecca Williamson is gratefully acknowledged—we couldn't have done the book without them or Holly Bell, Karen Butler, and other acquisitions and publishing professionals at Sopris West Educational Services who made our work better ... despite our frequent pleas to "leave it alone."

We also are indebted to Kate Algozzine and her outstanding team of research assistants (Leah Davis, Maggie Jaus, Hope Schweitzer, Kelley Taylor) at the Behavior and Reading Improvement Center at the University of North Carolina at Charlotte for their assistance in tracking down original sources for some of the strategies that we have included. This book was a collaborative effort, and it speaks for both of us.

M. L.

B. A.

ABOUT THE AUTHORS

Monica Lambert, Ed.D.

Monica Lambert is an assistant professor of special education in the Department of Language, Reading, and Exceptionalities at Appalacian State University in Boone, North Carolina. Her areas of expertise include learning disabilities, attention deficit disorder, cognitive and metacognitive strategies, teaching practices, and mathematics.

Dr. Lambert has extensive experience in teaching classroom management, methods, assessment, and learning disabilities courses; offers extensive staff development for LEAs; and advises students. She has published her research in a variety of special education journals. She is certified in learning strategies instruction and has conducted local, state, and national workshops on improving skills of students with learning disabilities using learning strategies.

Dr. Lambert uses her seven years of experience from teaching elementary, middle, and high school students with learning disabilities to enhance her courses and research.

Bob Algozzine, Ph.D.

Bob Algozzine is a professor in the Department of Educational Leadership and Co-Project Director for the OSEP-funded Behavior and Reading Improvement Center at the University of North Carolina at Charlotte. Dr. Algozzine has extensive experience in teaching introductory special education and behavior management courses, offers frequent staff development for LEAs, and advises students in a variety of graduate programs. He recently completed a nine-year tenure as one of two lead editors of *Exceptional Children*, the flagship journal of the Council for Exceptional Children.

Dr. Algozzine maintains active contact with the local public school system and served on the task force that was responsible for the current special education programs being implemented in the Charlotte-Mecklenburg Schools. He has published more than 250 manuscripts on a variety of topics in special education and has provided numerous professional development workshops on improving behavior and reading performance as well.

Dr. Algozzine has 25 years of research experience on broad issues in special education. He has taught students classified as seriously emotionally disturbed—and other clinically nebulous terms—and has authored books and textbooks that describe methods for managing emotional and social behavior problems. Dr. Algozzine is a requested speaker for professional development conferences on behavior management and other aspects of improving the lives of teachers and children.

CONTENTS

𝕾𝕰𝕮𝕿𝕴𝕺𝕹 3—What Now?

PREFACE

Strategies That Make Learning Fun (STMLF) is a book about learning strategies. Learning strategies are ways of organizing and using skills to learn content or accomplish other goals necessary for being successful in school. They are often represented by the first letters of key words that describe what students do or by using other acronyms or mnemonics to make them easy to remember. Frankly, we think STMLF (**Strategies That Make Learning Fun**) makes as much sense for the title of our book about learning strategies as FIST or POSSE make sense for titles of reading strategies, PLEASE makes sense for the title of a writing strategy, or LISTEN makes sense for the title of a social skills strategy. **WHYNOT** (**We Hope You Notice Our Thought**)?

In another bit of seemingly unorthodox writing, we begin and end each chapter with a quote from *World History According to College Students: Non Campus Mentis*, a great little book of historical "facts ... culled from term papers and bluebook exams written by college and university students" (Hendrickson 2001, p. viii). We decided to do this for two reasons:

1. We think the quotes are great reminders that even when we are way "on" the educational career ladder (as in college and university classes), we can also be way "off."

2. We think the quotes are a fun way to draw you into and move you out of each chapter (reading, teaching, and learning should be fun!).

What Is in Strategies That Make Learning Fun?

There is no other book quite like STMLF. There are plenty of descriptions of learning strategies "in the literature," but there are no compilations of learning strategies presented in a format designed to encourage, support, and help professionals use them. STMLF contains nine chapters in three sections.

Section 1—What's All This About Learning Strategies? includes two baseline chapters: Chapter 1 provides an overview of learning strategies, and Chapter 2 presents tips for implementing learning strategies in classrooms. The overview defines learning strategies, presents general evidence on their effectiveness, and describes how to teach them. The tips include some general advice for teaching learning strategies, components of effective learning strategies, some examples of ways to make teaching learning strategies more effective, and a strategy for teaching learning strategies.

Section 2—Using Learning Strategies to Improve Skills includes five chapters that describe different types of learning strategies: Reading Skills Strategies, Written Expression Skills Strategies, Mathematics Skills Strategies, Study Skills Strategies, and Social Skills Strategies. Approximately 40 specific learning strategies are described using the same format. The individual(s) responsible for promoting the learning strategy, the name of the learning strategy, and the primary source for information about the learning strategy are identified. When, why, and how to use the learning strategy—as well as "Teaching Tips" and suggestions for "Putting Theory Into Practice"—are also presented. Specific examples of forms, planning sheets, or other materials that illustrate how to use the learning strategy are included. Our goal is to present enough information for you to understand, use, and find out more about the learning strategies that we have included.

Section 3—What Now? includes two chapters designed to help you make the most of what you have learned about learning strategies in other sections of the book.

In Chapter 8, we present a strategy for conducting workshops, examples of content and handouts for a Mathematics Skills Learning Strategies Workshop, and additional information you can share with others about learning strategies. We also include a separate book section, Blackline Masters for Overhead Transparencies, which correlates to the Mathematics Skills Learning Strategies Workshop. The material comes directly from workshops that we have conducted to teach teachers, school psychologists, parents, and other professionals about learning strategies. The material is "doctor-tested," and we are confident that you will find it very helpful if you ever want to conduct a learning strategies workshop of your own. In Chapter 9, we give some closing thoughts and suggestions that provide a logical wrap-up to the book.

The big buzzwords in education today are "evidence-based practices," "bridging the research-to-practice gap," and "proven practices." They represent the latest answers to pleas to improve American education—usually presented after evidence of poor student performance is made public. Evidence-based practices (and similar catchphrases) are concerned more with use than with theory; they reflect a call for actions more than possibilities, promises, or speculations. We want this book to serve as an indispensable resource for people who are interested in evidence-based practices for organizing and using skills to learn content or in accomplishing other goals necessary for student academic and social success. We want this book to be the first source people turn to when they want to learn about learning strategies. We have organized and written the book so you can easily retrieve and apply the evidence-based practices described in it.

Who Is Strategies That Make Learning Fun *for?*

We wrote this book for professionals who are interested in finding effective ways to keep students actively involved in their own learning. We see this book as a primary medium for bringing selected evidence-based practices to practitioners. STMLF is for administrators, teachers (practicing and preservice), school psychologists, counselors, and parents. STMLF is a resource for anyone interested in learning more about learning strategies.

And, of course ... WHYEOW (<u>We</u> <u>H</u>ope <u>Y</u>ou <u>E</u>njoy <u>O</u>ur <u>W</u>ork).

SECTION 1

What's All This About Learning Strategies?

CHAPTER 1

WHO? WHAT? WHY? HOW?

As students shift from learning skills from teachers in early elementary grades to independently mastering academic content in later elementary, middle, and secondary grades, they face greater and greater demands to read information from textbooks, take notes from lectures, work independently, and express understanding in written compositions and on paper and pencil tests (Mercer & Mercer, 1985; Miller & Mercer, 1993; Schumaker & Deshler, 1984).

For students who have not developed such important academic skills, the task of learning content often comes with failure, particularly in general education classes where many students have acquired them. In response to this challenge, many students with learning problems—including those with learning disabilities (LD)—have acquired and used specific learning strategies to become successful despite their knowledge and skill deficits.

What Are Learning Strategies?

According to Davidson and Smith (1990), learning strategies are those methods employed by learners to facilitate their acquisition of knowledge and skills. Learning strategies are self-activated by the individual rather than being activated by the instructor and are used to encode and retrieve information from memory. In other words, students use self-generated strategies to support the processing of information while learning. These strategies represent complex mental operations that assist learners in all stages of information processing, such as perception, storage, retention, and recall. These techniques are behaviors as well as thought processes exercised during instruction and learning activities.

Learning strategies can be:

1. Mental techniques for organizing and elaborating on knowledge;
2. Active study strategies, such as taking notes in a particular way; or
3. General procedures for coping with learning problems associated with successful performance in school.

> History, a record of things left behind by past generations, started in 1815. Thus, we should try to view historical times as the behind of the present.

Simply put, a learning strategy is an individual's approach to completing a task. More specifically, a learning strategy is an individual's way of organizing and using a particular set of skills in order to learn content or accomplish other tasks more effectively and efficiently in school as well as in other settings (Schumaker & Deshler, 1992). Therefore, teachers who teach learning strategies teach students how to learn in addition to teaching them specific curriculum content or specific academic information.

Are Learning Strategies Effective?

In general, the use of learning strategies can improve student performance in classroom settings and on grade-appropriate tasks. In reading, for example, results from a study of the use of the Word Identification Strategy indicated that the number of oral reading errors decreased while reading comprehension scores increased for all students on ability-level and grade-level materials (Lenz & Hughes, 1990). Another study revealed that students using the Test Taking Strategy improved average test scores in inclusive classes from 57% to 71% (Hughes & Schumaker, 1991). Hughes, Ruhl, Schumaker, and Deshler (2002) found that homework performance improved when students used an "assignment completion strategy (PROJECT)."

Other researchers in the area of learning strategies have also found positive results. For example, Graham, Harris, MacArthur, and Schwartz (1991) have validated strategies for improving the quality of student compositions, planning processes, and revisions. In another line of research, Palincsar and Brown (1986) successfully tested and replicated reciprocal teaching, a strategy to improve student reading performance. Scruggs and Mastropieri (1992) have validated several approaches to teaching students how to construct and use mnemonics. Strategies tested by Miller and Mercer (1993) resulted in improved student performance in math calculations as well as in solving word problems. In a summary of research demonstrating "what works" in special education, memory aids and cognitive strategies were among the most effective interventions (Forness, Kavale, Blum, & Lloyd, 1997).

How Do You Teach Learning Strategies?

Educators at the University of Kansas, Center for Research on Learning, have validated an instructional sequence in which students learn each strategy following these teacher-directed steps: (a) Pretest; (b) Describe; (c) Model; (d) Verbal practice; (e) Controlled practice; (f) Grade-appropriate practice; (g) Posttest; and (h) Generalization (Schumaker & Deshler, 1992).

After a teacher assesses the current level of student performance on a strategy pretest, students commit to learning a new strategy. The teacher then describes the characteristics of the strategy and when, where, why, and how the strategy is used. Next, the teacher models how to use the strategy by "thinking aloud" as the strategy is applied to content material. During the verbal practice step, students memorize the strategy steps and other critical use requirements.

Afterward, controlled practice activities enable students to become proficient strategy users with ability-level materials. Teachers provide specific feedback on performance, and then students use the strategy with grade-appropriate or increasingly more difficult materials. Finally, after a posttest, teachers facilitate student generalization of strategy use in other academic and nonacademic settings.

Each strategy has multiple parts that students remember with the aid of a mnemonic. For example, in the Paraphrasing Strategy (Schumaker, Denton, & Deshler, 1984) students learn a reading comprehension strategy that is remembered by the acronym RAP:

> **R** = **R**ead a paragraph.
>
> **A** = **A**sk yourself, "What were the main idea and details in this paragraph?"
>
> **P** = **P**ut the main idea and details into your own words.

If students need to learn prerequisite skills, such as finding main ideas and details, teachers teach those before teaching the strategy and reinforce student mastery of those skills during strategy instruction. Students typically learn to use a learning strategy in small groups, sometimes in a resource room, through short, intensive lessons over several weeks.

What Is STMLF?

STMLF (*Strategies That Make Learning Fun*) is a resource for professionals who are interested in using learning strategies to improve academic and social performance of all students. Selected learning strategies are described in the following areas: reading skills, written expression skills, mathematics skills, study skills, and social skills. Selection was based on the following criteria:

- The strategy was widely represented in the learning strategies literature (e.g., FIST, QAR); or
- The strategy represented an evidence-based foundation practice in the learning strategies literature.

Not all learning strategies ever developed or demonstrated to be effective are included in this collection. Representative learning strategies in key skill areas are described using a common format (i.e., Who, What, Where, When, Why, and How). Teaching tips are included for each learning strategy. Details of use in "putting theory into practice" and sample materials are also included when doing so extends the practical level of presentation of particular learning strategies.

STMLF also includes a sample Mathematics Skills Learning Strategies Workshop—and a corresponding Blackline Masters for Overhead Transparencies book section—handouts, and additional materials needed for sharing information about learning strategies with others (Chapter 8). This chapter is not a substitute for professional training in the use of learning strategies, but more a simple, systematic, structured presentation of useful information for individuals interested in talking with colleagues, students, and parents about learning strategies.

My brain is on hold, so I can't remember much. So without further adieu, let's get to the research!

Information in this chapter is based primarily on a public domain document entitled, "Learning Strategies," which was prepared by Daniel J. Boudah and Kevin J. O'Neill under the Contract No. ED-99-CO-0026 between the Educational Resources Information Center (ERIC) Clearinghouse on Disabilities and Gifted Education and the U.S. Department of Education, Office of Special Education Programs (OSEP). The opinions expressed in that report do not necessarily reflect the positions of the policies of OSEP or the Department of Education. ERIC/OSEP Digests are in the public domain and may be freely reproduced and disseminated; the content of the original publication was modified slightly and updated here to conform to the style and format of the rest of the publication.

TIPS FOR USING LEARNING STRATEGIES IN THE CLASSROOM

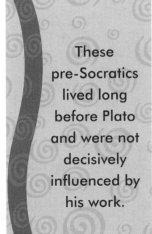 There is plenty of advice available on how to teach learning strategies. We provide some examples of guidelines and steps that appear frequently in the literature on learning strategies. We also provide a description of what makes learning strategies effective, some tips for helping students remember strategy steps, and (of course!) a strategy for teaching learning strategies.

General Advice for Teaching Learning Strategies

Guidelines for how to teach students to use learning strategies are available (Clark, Deshler, Schumaker, Alley, & Warner, 1984; Ellis, Deshler, Lenz, Schumaker, & Clark, 1991; Ellis, Lenz, & Sabornie, 1987a, 1987b). Generally, the steps include:

1. Allowing students to perform a task without instruction to assess their skill levels.
2. Helping students understand the problems associated with their current strategies.
3. Explaining the new strategy and its advantages as compared with students' existing strategies.
4. Demonstrating the strategy for students.
5. Teaching students to rehearse the strategy verbally.
6. Providing students with opportunities to practice the new strategy.
7. Offering feedback on the students' use of the new strategy.
8. Evaluating students to ensure their mastery of the new strategy.

These pre-Socratics lived long before Plato and were not decisively influenced by his work.

Davidson and Smith (1990) provide an example of using strategy instruction to teach high school students in content-area classes—a note-taking technique that involves the use of graphic organizers representing typical text structures found in expository prose (e.g., chronology, cause-effect, and problem-solution). Although especially useful for low-ability students, average and above-average students also find this Note-Taking Strategy helps them understand and retain information in content-area reading materials. The instructional procedure involves the following steps:

1. *Gain attention, inform learner of the objective, and stimulate recall of prior knowledge.* A reading passage is assigned and students are asked to read and study it as they normally would. After they have read the material, the teacher leads a discussion about what the students did and the outcome(s) of it. The objective of the new instructional procedure (i.e., learning a note-taking strategy) is presented.

   Purposes for taking notes are discussed and students are encouraged to share other note-taking techniques and problems that they have in taking notes. The teacher points out that having trouble deciding what to include or how to organize notes is common, and students are told that they will be learning a strategy that may help them when taking notes.

   The teacher tells students that effort and just "trying hard" will sometimes lead to success. The teacher also points out that success in learning requires the use of appropriate strategies for completing assignments and demonstrating that the material has been learned.

   Finally, the teacher reviews the content structures and the graphical representations that students learned in earlier lessons. The structures include time-order, comparison-contrast, problem-solution, problem-solution-results, cause-effect, description, and definition-example.

2. *Present reading materials and guide learning.* The teacher points out that this Note-Taking Strategy is appropriate for expository rather than narrative reading assignments, reviewing the concept "expository" with explanations as required (i.e., *expository* text explains something using definitions, sequenced material, categories, comparing and contrasting, listing, illustrating, and presenting solutions, descriptions, or cause-effect relations; a *narrative* text includes a theme, a plot, conflict[s], resolution, characters, and a setting). Whereas the narrative text uses story to inform and persuade, the expository text uses facts and details, opinions, and examples to inform or explain.

   The teacher also states that this strategy is most appropriate when the learning task is to "understand" main ideas and interrelationships of ideas, rather than to recall isolated facts. The usefulness of the Note-Taking Strategy over writing long passages or recopying less-structured notes is then discussed. This strategy may also be compared to the more widely known strategy of outlining, and the types of assignments and purposes for which the new strategy and the outlining strategy are appropriate might be discussed.

3. *Elicit performance and provide feedback.* The teacher provides sample assignments for students to use in deciding whether the Note-Taking Strategy is appropriate to use (passages requiring identification of main ideas and their interrelationships to other ideas are appropriate). Explanations of correct answers are used for supportive feedback, and corrective feedback is provided to reduce the likelihood of incorrect answers in the future.

4. *Present the stimulus materials and guide learning.* Thinking aloud all the steps in the learning strategy, the teacher demonstrates how to use it, including showing how it is appropriate to the task. The steps in the strategy may be presented in a checklist for later use:

USING THE NOTE-TAKING STRATEGY	✔
• The assignment requires fitting ideas together.	❏
• The assignment requires more than remembering isolated facts.	❏
• The assignment includes expository text.	❏
• Skim text to identify main idea(s) and structure of content presented.	❏
• Use a picture to show the main idea(s) and structure of the text.	❏
• Read the text to confirm and illustrate the structure and main idea(s).	❏
• Check comprehension by recalling how ideas in text relate to each other.	❏
• Scan the text if comprehension is weak.	❏

5. *Elicit performance, provide feedback.* The teacher has students list the steps in the strategy in the correct order and offers feedback to support appropriate recall in the future.

6. *Present stimulus materials, guide learning.* The teacher models the Note-Taking Strategy using a "think aloud" procedure and expository text (three to five paragraphs) from a content-area textbook. First, the teacher states a purpose for reading the material and scans the passage to identify main idea(s) and structure of content presented. As the teacher works through the text, he or she talks about how the structure relates to the content presentation and clarifies misunderstandings as they become evident. The teacher scans forward and backward frequently to confirm that ideas support the main idea(s) and structure that have been identified. After reading the passage completely, the main idea(s) and structure are represented in graphic form. The graphic summary is confirmed using the text and adding pictorial cues to represent main idea(s) or important details. Paraphrasing rather than exact wording are used when filling in the graphic representation.

7. *Elicit performance, provide feedback.* The teacher provides students with both an explicitly cued and an implicitly cued passage of expository text (three to five paragraphs each). The teacher breaks students into pairs for practice using the Note-Taking Strategy, starting with the explicitly cued passage. One student reads the passage aloud, describes his or her thought processes, and takes notes while the other student provides feedback and encouragement using the checklist. Students switch roles and use the same procedures for the implicitly cued passage.

8. *Present stimulus materials, guide learning.* The teacher introduces a complete assignment of expository material (e.g., an entire chapter) that has explicit and clear structures and again models the Note-Taking Strategy. The teacher may underline or create marginal notes to highlight structure and use a graphic organizer to illustrate combinations of structures. The teacher reminds students that different organizers can be developed to illustrate the structures in the passage.

9. *Elicit performance, provide feedback.* Students are provided with chapter-length, explicitly cued, and cleanly structured expository material like they used before. Again working in pairs, students generate a graphic organizer using what they have learned. The teacher collects and reviews their work and discusses and evaluates two or three in a subsequent lesson. In the discussion, the teacher provides feedback on selection of structures, layout on page, selection of main ideas, and details included on the organizer. Students then complete a similar activity independently.

10. *Assess performance.* The teacher tests students by having them use the Note-Taking Strategy independently. The teacher observes students' performance as they complete the task and collects their notes and reviews them for accuracy. The teacher then discusses the performance of each student independently. With this Note-Taking Strategy, performance could also be tested using videotaped or audiotaped sessions.

11. *Enhance retention and transfer.* To promote transfer, the teacher models use of the Note-Taking Strategy with implicitly structured and poorly organized materials. Students are shown alternative structures that might be used in creating graphic organizers, and they discuss how selection of alternate structures emphasizes different points. To facilitate understanding and generalization, students practice the Note-Taking Strategy with implicitly organized and poorly organized chapter-length materials.

What Makes Learning Strategies Effective?

This resource, presented in STMLF design format, documents a description of what makes learning strategies effective.

Components of Effective Learning Strategies

Who: Edwin S. Ellis and B. Keith Lenz

What: Components of Effective Learning Strategies

Where: Ellis, E.S. & Lenz, B.K. (1987). A component analysis of effective learning strategies for LD students. *Learning Disabilities Focus, 2,* 94–107.

When: There is a need to evaluate strategies being considered for development.

Why: Success of any implementation of new learning strategies is dependent on the extent to which principles of effective instruction are followed.

How: Selected learning strategies are described to illustrate how learning strategies help students learn by emphasizing the following skills:

1. **Rehearsal Strategies.** Reciting silently or orally, or reviewing images visually, facilitates remembering.

2. **Transformational Strategies.** Changing, embellishing, or elaborating information helps students remember.

3. **Organizational Strategies.** Manipulating information facilitates memory.

4. **Mnemonic Strategies.** Using key words or first-letter memory aids makes learning successful.

5. **Monitoring Strategies.** Consistent and continuing checking of progress facilitates success.

6. **Motivational Strategies.** Self-coping and self-reinforcement facilitate learning.

The best manner for introducing steps of learning strategies is illustrated using the following critical characteristics:

1. The packaging of the learning strategy is simple and brief. Most learning strategies involve between three and seven steps.

2. The packaging of the learning strategy is characterized by a remembering system that facilitates recall. Learning strategies are represented using acronyms or abbreviations that cue students on what to do and what to do next.

3 Instruction in a learning strategy is dependent on skills and needs of students. Identifying skills necessary to be successful is essential to the effective use of learning strategies.

4. The presentation of a learning strategy should address limitations. When to use and when not to use a learning strategy should be identified to help students avoid frustration.

5. The learning strategy is presented using principles of effective learning. Modeling, using reinforcement, shaping, and demonstrating mastery make a difference in efforts to teach learning strategies.

Helping Students Remember Strategy Steps

This resource, also presented in STMLF design format, documents ideas for helping students remember strategy steps.

Using Picture Symbols

Who: Sandra McCandless Simmons

What: Using Picture Symbols

Where: Simmons, S.M. (1989). PSRT—A reading comprehension strategy. *Journal of Reading, 32*(5), 419–427.

When: Helping students to remember steps in a strategy being used.

Why: Students often need assistance in remembering what they are learning. An effective way to remind students of the steps in a learning strategy is by associating a picture or symbol with each step.

How: PSRT is a Reading Comprehension Strategy. To use it, students need to remember an action represented by each letter:

P = **Prepare:** Find out what students already know.

S = **Structure:** Help students see how the text is organized.

R = **Read:** Have students read the text.

T = **Think:** Discuss the text.

One way to remember the steps in this strategy is to use the abbreviation PSRT. When students need an additional reminder, assign a picture or symbol to each step. For example, the **Prepare** step could be represented with a question mark (?) picture symbol; the **Structure** step could be represented with a diagram symbol (reflecting stages in a process); the **Read** step could be represented with a picture of a person reading a book; and the **Think** step could be represented with a picture of thinkers asking questions (see "Putting Theory Into Practice" section).

Teaching Tips

- Choose a learning strategy for use with picture symbols.
- Associate a picture with each separate step in the strategy.
- Draw a picture next to the step on an index card and practice the strategy with the card in view.
- Use the pictures without the words associated with them to practice the steps of the strategy.
- Practice the strategy without using the picture symbols.

Putting Theory into Practice

Perceptual cueing may help students learn other strategies. Use the information below as a handout to remind students to:

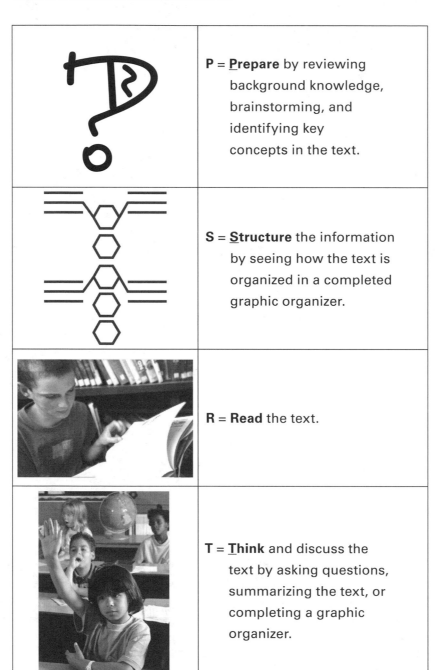

	P = **Prepare** by reviewing background knowledge, brainstorming, and identifying key concepts in the text.
	S = **Structure** the information by seeing how the text is organized in a completed graphic organizer.
	R = **Read** the text.
	T = **Think** and discuss the text by asking questions, summarizing the text, or completing a graphic organizer.

Everybody Agrees

Teaching students strategies to use when studying, taking tests, or reading in content-area textbooks can be highly effective in improving overall achievement, performance, and outcomes. The model for teaching students to use learning strategies is simple.

1. *Assess levels of existing skills.* Give a pretest to identify current levels of functioning and to establish a baseline for measuring future performance. Use this information to illustrate the need for improving particular skills and for using specific learning strategies.

2. *Describe a strategy for improving performance.* Give an overview of the strategy, informing students of goals, steps, and relations to skills needing improvement. Focus students' attention on reasons why the strategy will be helpful in improving their performance.

3. *Demonstrate the strategy.* Give students an active demonstration of the steps of the strategy. Tell them everything they need to know to be successful with the strategy.

4. *Practice.* Give students opportunities to demonstrate the steps of the learning strategy before having them practice independently. Once you are sure they have mastered the basics, have them use the strategy to complete appropriate assignments.

5. *Control practice.* Give assignments that allow students to practice the learning strategy in material that is at their current performance level. Try to achieve high rates of success (e.g., 90%) in these controlled assignments.

6. *Advance practice.* Give assignments that allow students to practice the learning strategy in higher-level material at grade-level if possible. One goal of using strategies is to improve performance, and this often requires working with challenging material.

7. *Assess levels of developing skills.* Give students opportunities to demonstrate what they have learned. Compare performance before and after using learning strategies to evaluate the effectiveness of the instructional sequence.

8. *Generalize skills.* Give students assignments that require use of learning strategies in different settings or content. Generalizing the use of learning strategies to different classrooms or instructional materials is an excellent indication of success.

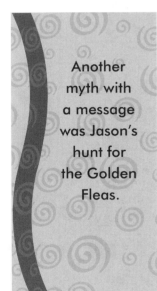

Another myth with a message was Jason's hunt for the Golden Fleas.

We suggest you use our STRATEGY Strategy to teach strategies. The steps are self-explanatory:

S = **Start** with an appraisal of current functioning, and identify a strategy to improve it.

T = **Teach** the strategy using specific, direct instruction.

R = **Rehearse** and model each component of the strategy often.

A = **Arrange** practice sessions with controlled materials.

T = **Try** the strategy with actual classroom materials.

E = **Engage** in frequent feedback.

G = **Give** frequent opportunities to use the strategy.

Y = **Yield** evaluation data after using the strategy.

SECTION 2

Using Learning Strategies to Improve Skills

READING SKILLS STRATEGIES

Critical Thinking Map

Who: Lorna Idol

What: Critical Thinking Map

Where: Idol, L. (1987). A critical thinking map to improve content area comprehension of poor readers. *Remedial and Special Education, 8,* 28–40.

When: When students have difficulty understanding what they have read.

Why: Many times, teachers who teach very poor readers to read tend to focus more on word recognition than on reading comprehension. Reading comprehension can be improved by teaching students to impose a structure on the text so that they learn to think as they read.

How: Have students complete a story map that includes the following components (also *see* A Map for Critical Thinking) during or after reading a textbook passage:

> **Important Events**
>
> **Main Idea/Lesson**
>
> **Other Viewpoints/Opinions**
>
> **Reader's Conclusions**
>
> **Relevance to Today**

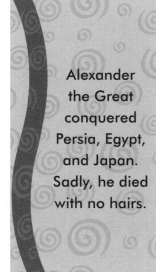

Alexander the Great conquered Persia, Egypt, and Japan. Sadly, he died with no hairs.

Teaching Tips

- Clarify the purposes (explicit and implicit) for any reading activity.
- Identify important aspects of the passage.
- Focus on the primary content rather than trivial aspects of it.
- Monitor students frequently to determine their levels of comprehension.
- Use self-questioning to determine if progress is being made.
- Quickly correct problems in comprehension to prevent long-term consequences.

Putting Theory Into Practice

Idol (p. 39) provides the following steps for "teachers interested in teaching their students to use critical thinking maps":

Step 1: Have the student read several passages silently and answer five generic questions after reading each of them:

   a. What is the main idea?

   b. What facts support the main idea?

   c. What are some other points of view about this topic?

   d. What is your conclusion?

   e. How is this passage relevant to a modern problem?

Step 2: Use data from the silent reading of passages to decide if the student needs to learn to use a critical thinking map (students who score 60% [or lower] correct need assistance).

Step 3: Show a critical thinking map (*see* A Map for Critical Thinking) to the student and provide examples of what is meant by each component.

   a. Important events are points, steps, or happenings that lead to the main idea of the passage. They are usually explicit statements. Sometimes, they are presented in a "compare and contrast" format, and other times they are represented in a list.

   b. The main idea is the most important information presented in the passage. Sometimes, there is more than one main idea presented in a lesson or a textbook passage.

   c. Other viewpoints and opinions are identified by asking the reader to: (1) Identify information that is missing; (2) State other ways to present the information; or (3) Relate what he or she already knows about the topic reflected in the passage.

   d. The reader's conclusions reflect integration of what is known with what has been read.

   e. Relevance to today is based on making comparisons between past and present information.

Step 4: For two lessons, model the strategy by: (1) Noting the number of pages to be read; (2) Reading the passage aloud, interrupting your reading as you identify components; and (3) Filling in the components on a critical thinking map. After reading the entire passage aloud, orally reread the map components, checking for accuracy and adjusting the map content if more information is needed.

Step 5: Have the student read a passage silently. After the passage has been read, lead the student in looking for information to complete the critical thinking map.

Step 6: Take the completed map from the student and have him or her complete written responses to the five generic questions presented in Step 1. Correct the written product.

Step 7: Provide feedback on the student's responses. Discuss discrepancies between incorrect comprehension responses and correct critical thinking map information. Have the student rewrite incorrect responses to the comprehension questions.

Step 8: Ask the student to fill in critical thinking maps with less and less assistance.

Step 9: When comprehension responses consistently remain above 80% correct with little or no assistance, discontinue use of the critical thinking map.

Step 10: To challenge a student, stop using the five generic questions. After silently reading a textbook passage, have the student write a paragraph that includes each component of the critical thinking map.

A MAP FOR CRITICAL THINKING

Name_____ Chapter _____ Part _____

Date _____ Phase _____

Important Events, Points, or Steps

```
┌─────────────────────────────────────────────────────┐
│                                                     │
│                                                     │
│                                                     │
└─────────────────────────────────────────────────────┘
```

Main Idea/Lesson

```
┌─────────────────────────────────────────────────────┐
│                                                     │
│                                                     │
│                                                     │
└─────────────────────────────────────────────────────┘
```

Other Viewpoints/Opinions

```
┌─────────────────────────────────────────────────────┐
│                                                     │
│                                                     │
│                                                     │
└─────────────────────────────────────────────────────┘
```

Reader's Conclusions

```
┌─────────────────────────────────────────────────────┐
│                                                     │
│                                                     │
│                                                     │
└─────────────────────────────────────────────────────┘
```

Relevance to Today

```
┌─────────────────────────────────────────────────────┐
│                                                     │
│                                                     │
│                                                     │
└─────────────────────────────────────────────────────┘
```

(Idol, 1987, p. 30)

FIST

Who: Edwin S. Ellis and B. Keith Lenz

What: FIST

Where: Ellis, E.S. & Lenz, B.K. (1987). A component analysis of effective learning strategies for LD students. *Learning Disabilities Focus, 2*, 97–101. *

When: Students have difficulties comprehending reading materials.

Why: To improve reading comprehension. The strategy teaches students to self-question and paraphrase as they read.

How: F = <u>F</u>irst sentence in the paragraph is read.

I = <u>I</u>ndicate a question based on information in the first sentence.

S = <u>S</u>earch for the answer to the question.

T = <u>T</u>ie the answer to the question with a paraphrase.

Teaching Tips

- Teach students to paraphrase before teaching FIST.
- Use the STRATEGY Strategy (*see* Chapter 2, p. 16) to teach.
- Begin teaching FIST with short paragraphs, then use longer reading passages.
- Use the FIST Worksheet.

* Also described in Clark, F.L., Warner, M.M., Alley, G.R., Deshler, D.D., Schumaker, J.B., Vetter, A.F., & Nolan, S.M. (1981). *Visual imagery and self-questioning: Strategies to improve comprehension of written material* (Research Report #51). Lawrence, KS: University of Kansas Institute for Research in Learning Disabilities.

Putting Theory Into Practice

Teach students the FIST steps by describing each one. In the first step, students read the first sentence of a paragraph. In the second step, students create a question about the first sentence. The third and fourth steps are combined as students state the answer in a paraphrase.

The FIST Worksheet can be used to monitor student use and progress with the strategy. Several worksheets can be duplicated on one page.

FIST WORKSHEET

I read the first sentence. _____

My question is: _____

_____

The answer in my own words: _____

_____

_____

Five-Step Reading Comprehension Strategy

Who: Dale H. Schunk and Jo Mary Rice

What: Five-Step Reading Comprehension Strategy

Where: Schunk, D.H. & Rice, J.M. (1986). Extended attributional feedback: Sequence effects during remedial reading instruction. *Journal of Early Adolescence, 5,* 247–258.

Schunk, D.H. & Rice, J.M. (1987). Enhancing comprehension skill and self-efficacy with strategy value information. *Journal of Reading Behavior, 19,* 285–302.

When: Students need a strategy to assist them in understanding a story or passage of connected text.

Why: Explicit instruction on effective reading comprehension strategies has important effects on formal and informal performance assessments at all grade levels.

How: When students are presented with reading passages followed by multiple-choice comprehension questions, they ask themselves the question, "What do I have to do?" Then, students answer that question with the strategy sequence:

1. Read the question.

2. Read the passage to find out what it is mostly about.

3. Think about what the details have in common.

4. Think about what would make a good title.

5. Reread the story if I don't know the answer to the question.

Teaching Tips

• Display the Five-Step Reading Comprehension Strategy on a poster board in the classroom.

• Before and after students read a passage, provide information about the value of using the strategy:

"Using steps like these should help you whenever you have to answer questions about something you have read." (Students may find that using these steps will help them whenever they have to answer questions about passages they have read.)

"Using steps like these should help you whenever you have to answer questions about main ideas." (Students may find that using these steps will help them whenever they have to answer questions about main ideas.)

- When students correctly answer comprehension questions after using the strategy, provide strategy effectiveness feedback to enhance the value of what they are doing:

    "You got it right because you followed the steps we are learning in the right order."

    "Answering questions is easier when you follow the steps."

    "You have been correctly answering a lot more questions since you started using the steps."

POSSE

Who: Carol Sue Englert and Troy Mariage

What: POSSE

Where: Englert, C.S. & Mariage, T. (1990). Send for the POSSE: Structuring the comprehension dialogue. *Academic Therapy, 25,* 473–487.

When: Students have difficulty comprehending reading materials.

Why: Reading comprehension is improved when students predict ideas based on their own background knowledge, organize ideas presented in reading passages, and use different approaches to summarize and evaluate what they have read.

How: P = **P**redict which ideas are in the story (what the passage is about).

O = **O**rganize knowledge into categories (how content is presented).

S = **S**earch for text structure (what main ideas and details are included).

S = **S**ummarize in your own words (what the passage means to you).

E = **E**valuate by asking, comparing, clarifying, and predicting questions.

Teaching Tips

- Use the STRATEGY Strategy (*see* Chapter 2, p. 16) to teach.
- Think of three stages when teaching and learning to use the POSSE Strategy:

  1. Prereading (**P**redict and **O**rganize)

  2. Reading (**S**earch)

  3. Postreading (**S**ummarize and **E**valuate)
- Begin teaching POSSE with short stories, then use longer stories.

Putting Theory Into Practice

Background knowledge is important in understanding connected text and informational passages such as those typically included in content-area textbooks. The POSSE Strategy begins by having students use cues provided in the title, headings, tables, figures, graphs, beginning paragraph, or other parts of the story to **Predict** what it will be about based on what they already know about the topic(s). During this prereading stage, the teacher encourages students to freely express their ideas. Teachers often ask questions like, "What do you think this story/passage will be about?" or "What parts of the story/passage will help you make predictions about the content that is going to be presented?" Teachers also often act as scribes in recording student responses on a strategy sheet (*see* the POSSE Strategy Sheet).

During the second prereading stage, students **Organize** their predictions from the first stage by grouping them into categories likely to be included in the passage. Semantic mapping is an effective way to classify and group the predictions. After the information has been organized, the teacher asks students to identify gaps in their knowledge base that may be filled by reading the passage.

During the reading stage, students **Search** for ideas and details to confirm their predictions. They read to identify the actual categories used by the author to present information in the passage, and they record their findings.

After reading the passage, students **Summarize** the main idea of the passage and identify details that support it (*see* the Sample Dialogue). The teacher sometimes helps students to begin summarizing by pointing out that the main idea is what the paragraph is all about and that it is usually supported by a series of ideas, facts, or details that can be identified and written down.

In the final step after reading the passage, students **Evaluate** their understanding of the passage. Questions about the main idea or supporting details (e.g., Who? What? Where? When? Why? How?) are posed and answered; comparisons of predicted and actual content of the passage are completed; questions about unfamiliar vocabulary, unclear information, or unknown facts are clarified; and predictions about subsequent paragraphs, passages, or parts are proposed.

POSSE STRATEGY SHEET

Predict   *What information will be presented in the passage?*

_____

_____

_____

_____

Organize   *How do you think the information will be presented?*

Search   *How was the information presented?*

Summarize   *What was the main idea of the passage?*

_____

What details help you to know what the passage is all about?

_____

_____

_____

Evaluate   *What helps you understand the passage?*

Questions?_____

Compare?_____

Clarify? _____

Predict?_____

Sample Dialogue for <u>Summarize</u> Step of the POSSE Strategy

Teacher	"Do you think the saving of the soldier's dog is the main idea?"
Charles:	"No. I think it is the mother looking back to the war and having memories of the war."
Teacher:	"And the dog might have been a detail rather than the main idea?"
Charles:	"Yes. The mother says, 'What I remember best is the soldier with the dog.' Now that is from here to here (pointing to passage). And all of this up here (pointing) is about the other memories. So it is the total memories."
Teacher:	"I agree. When we talk about the dog, that is a detail rather than the main idea. A main idea is an idea that runs through a paragraph and is supported by the total set of facts. There are many supporting ideas for the mother's memories, but there is only one idea related to the soldier's dog."

(Englert & Mariage, pp. 483–484)

Question-Answer Relationship (QAR)

Who: Taffy E. Raphael

What: Question-Answer Relationship (QAR) (four types)

Where: Raphael, T.E. (1986). Teaching question-answering strategies for children. *The Reading Teacher, 39,* 516–523.

When: Students need a strategy to help with comprehension of stories.

Why: Students need to be aware of different question types in a story. Students need to comprehend a story.

How: 1. **Right There:** Find the answer in the story (literal and detail).

2. **Think and Search:** Look for the answer in several places.

3. **Author and You:** Make inferences and conclusions.

4. **On Your Own:** The answer must come from the reader's experience and knowledge.

Teaching Tips

• Use the STRATEGY Strategy (*see* Chapter 2, p. 16) to teach.

• Model the four types of QARs using visual cues.

• Begin teaching with a short text and progress to longer text.

• Guide students through the steps and move toward independence.

Putting Theory Into Practice

When teaching this strategy, it is important to teach the four types of QARs (refer to the QAR Strategy Chart). It may help students to add visual cues to remember the types. The teacher should model the strategy using a variety of reading passages. Begin with reading passages that will allow students to easily find the Question-Answer Relationships. This will assist them in understanding that some answers can easily be found **Right There** in the text. Some questions will require the reader to **Think and Search** for the answer. Other questions will require prior knowledge for the answer (**Author and You**), and some questions may be answered **On Your Own**.

Raphael suggests that the first two QAR types—**Right There** and **Think and Search**—be taught together, since they are both found in the story. The last two QAR types—**Author and You** and **On Your Own**—should also be taught together, since they are mental processes.

QAR Strategy Chart

1. **Right There** in the story.

2. **Think and Search** harder in the story to find the answer.

3. **Author and You** inferences.

4. **On Your Own**.

Reading Strategies for Older Students

Who: Susan Lebzelter and E. Jane Nowacek

What: Reading Strategies for Older Students

Where: Lebzelter, S. & Nowacek, E.J. (1999). Reading strategies for secondary students with mild disabilities. *Intervention in School and Clinic, 34,* 212–219.

When: Students reach a plateau in their overall reading skills.

Why: Teachers are often faced with questions about how to provide reading instruction that meets the needs of older students with learning problems.

How: Lebzelter and Nowacek (p. 217) provide brief descriptions of decoding strategies (DISSECT and WIST), vocabulary strategies (IT FITS, LINCS), and reading comprehension strategies (ASK IT, The Paraphrasing Strategy, Summarization Strategy) for use in improving the reading performance of older students. They also delimit steps needed to evaluate strategies that are being considered or used:

1. **Investigate the strategy content.**
   - Do the steps lead students toward a specific, positive outcome (e.g., passing a test)?
   - Are the steps of the strategy sequenced in a logical, efficient manner?
   - Do the steps cue students to use specific cognitive strategies?
   - Do the steps cue students to use metacognitive processes (e.g., checking, reviewing)?
   - Do the steps cue students to select and implement appropriate procedures, rules, and skills?
   - Do the steps cue students to take overt/physical actions?
   - Are these physical actions supported by a clear explanation of the mental actions that must be taken?
   - Can the steps be performed in a reasonably short time, and have unnecessary steps been deleted?
   - Does the instructional sequence specify why, when, and where the strategy is to be used?

2. **Review the strategy design.**
   - Are entry-level skills specified in some strategy steps?
   - Is there a simple, short memorization system to help students remember the strategy (e.g., a mnemonic word or image)?

- Does the first word of every step lead students toward a mental or physical action that will be taken?
- Does remembering the system or strategy consist of seven or fewer steps?
  - Is the system to memorize the strategy related to the strategy function?
  - Is the language used in the steps reader-friendly?
3. **Justify the usefulness of the strategy.**
  - Will the strategy be relevant to the settings in which students function?
  - Will the strategy be transferable to, and generalized in, a variety of settings and situations?
  - Does the strategy have potential for future use?

RIDER

Who: Edwin S. Ellis and B. Keith Lenz

What: RIDER

Where: Ellis, E.S. & Lenz, B.K. (1987). A component analysis of effective learning strategies for LD students. *Learning Disabilities Focus, 2,* 97–101. *

When: Students have difficulties comprehending reading materials.

Why: To improve reading comprehension. The strategy teaches students to visualize what they are reading.

How: R = **R**ead (the sentence).

I = **I**mage (make an image or a picture in your mind).

D = **D**escribe (describe how the new image is different from the previous sentence).

E = **E**valuate (as you make the image or picture, check to make sure it contains everything necessary).

R = **R**epeat (as you read the next sentence, repeat the RIDE steps).

Teaching Tips

• Use the STRATEGY Strategy (*see* Chapter 2, p. 16) to teach.

• Have students draw pictures to show what they are visualizing.

• Begin teaching RIDER with short paragraphs, then use longer reading passages.

• Interview students to determine if their images match the reading content.

* Also described in Clark, F.L., Warner, M.M., Alley, G.R., Deshler, D.D., Schumaker, J.B., Vetter, A.F., & Nolan, S.M. (1981). *Visual imagery and self-questioning*: Strategies to improve comprehension of written material (Research Report #51). Lawrence, KS: University of Kansas Institute for Research in Learning Disabilities.

Putting Theory Into Practice

In the first step of the strategy—**Read**—students read the first sentence (e.g., "Susie was walking home from school one day and found a cute, dark gray kitten playing in an empty field").

During the second step of the strategy—**Image**—teach students to create a visual picture of what they read. In this case, the image should include a girl, a field, and a kitten. Encourage students to think about what the girl, field, and kitten look like. The more detailed their images, the better students will remember what they read.

In the third step—**Describe**—students tell how the second sentence image is different from the first sentence image. For example, if the second sentence is, "Susie was so excited because she had always wanted a kitten," the new image might be of Susie with a cloud above her head, dreaming of a kitten. The image could also include Susie jumping up and down with excitement.

Evaluate—the fourth step—requires students to make sure they include everything necessary in their images (e.g., a girl, a field, and a kitten would be included in the first sentence image).

The last step requires students to **Repeat** the RIDE steps as they continue reading.

Summarization Strategy

Who: Beth E. Kurtz and John G. Borkowski

What: Summarization Strategy

Where: Kurtz, B.E. & Borkowski, J.G. (1987). Development of strategic skills in impulsive and reflective children: A longitudinal study of metacognition. *Journal of Experimental and Child Psychology, 43,* 129–148.

When: Students have difficulty summarizing paragraphs and locating the main idea.

Why: Content-area teachers rely on textbooks as a main source of instruction. To be successful in content-area courses, students have to be able to complete their reading assignments.

How: After reading a paragraph:

1. Identify the main idea sentence by asking, "What is this paragraph about?"

2. Identify the reason by asking, "Why?"

3. Combine the main idea and the reason into a summary statement.

Teaching Tips

- Use the STRATEGY Strategy (*see* Chapter 2, p. 16) to teach.

- Kurtz and Borkowski suggest, in the initial teaching, having students find a topic heading in a list of words or having them write a topic name for a list of words. This can lead into a discussion about how paragraphs have topics, main ideas, and supporting details.

- Use this strategy when finding the main idea and details in various types of paragraphs (e.g., descriptive, explanatory).

- Have students create a topic sentence for paragraphs that have the topic missing.

- Use the optional Prerequisite Activity and/or the Summarization Strategy Worksheet.

Putting Theory Into Practice

The teacher may want to conduct this optional Prerequisite Activity prior to using the Summarization Strategy Worksheet.

PREREQUISITE ACTIVITY FOR SUMMARIZATION STRATEGY

Directions: Find the best topic heading for the following list of words, and write it in the blank.

1. Topic _____

     Sand

     Ocean

     Shovel and pail

     Beach ball

     Sunscreen

     Towel

Topic heading choices: *"A Fun Day"*

                                "A Day at the Beach"

                                "Sam's Birthday"

2. Topic _____

     Ball and bat

     Catcher's mask

     Glove

     Popcorn and soda

     Stadium

Topic heading choices: *"A Football Game"*

                                "The Baseball Game"

                                "Going to a Game"

Use this worksheet to teach students how to summarize paragraphs.

SUMMARIZATION STRATEGY WORKSHEET

1. Begin by reading the paragraph.
2. Identify the main idea sentence by asking,
   "What is this paragraph about?"
   Write it down:

   _____

   _____

3. Identify the reason by asking, "Why?"
   Write it down:

   _____

   _____

4. Combine the main idea and the reason into a summary
   statement.
   Write it down:

   _____

   _____

   _____

YOU DID IT!

Plato invented reality. He was teacher to Harris Tottle, author of *The Republicans*

CHAPTER 4

WRITTEN EXPRESSION SKILLS STRATEGIES

C-SPACE

Who: Charles A. MacArthur, Shirley S. Schwartz, and Steve Graham

What: C-SPACE (to plan a story)

Where: MacArthur, C.A., Schwartz, S.S., & Graham, S. (1991). A model for writing instruction: Integrating word processing and strategy instruction into a process approach to writing. *Learning Disability Research & Practice, 6,* 230–236.

When: Students need a strategy to help them plan and write stories.

Why: Students often need help in the planning stage of writing.

How: C = <u>C</u>haracters

S = <u>S</u>etting

P = <u>P</u>roblem or <u>P</u>urpose

A = <u>A</u>ction

C = <u>C</u>onclusion

E = <u>E</u>motion

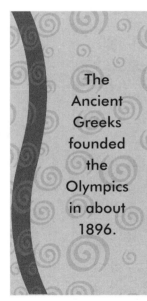

The Ancient Greeks founded the Olympics in about 1896.

Teaching Tips

- This strategy can be used with the TREE Strategy *(see* p. 44).
- Use the C-SPACE Planning Form.
- Model how to use this strategy and the planning form.
- Encourage the planning stage of writing by requiring and grading the planning form.
- Have a two- to three-minute conference with students to review the planning form before they write their stories.

C-SPACE Planning Form

Characters in the story:

_____ _____ _____ _____
_____ _____ _____ _____

Setting: _____
_____
_____

What is the **Problem** or **Purpose**? _____
_____

What is the **Action** in the story? _____
_____
_____
_____

Conclusion: _____
_____
_____
_____

What is the **Emotion** I want to get the reader to feel? _____
_____
_____
_____

DEFENDS

Who: Edwin S. Ellis and B. Keith Lenz

What: DEFENDS (a strategy for writing positions)

Where: Ellis, E.S. & Lenz, B.K. (1987). A component analysis of effective learning strategies for LD students. *Learning Disabilities Focus, 2*, 94–107.

When: Students need to write a position paper.

Why: Students often need to write a focused composition, especially in content-area courses.

How: Follow these steps:

D = **Decide** on exact position.

E = **Examine** the reasons for the position.

F = **Form** a list of points that explain each reason.

E = **Expose** your position in the first sentence.

N = **Note** each reason and supporting points.

D = **Drive** home the position in the last sentence.

S = **Search** for errors and correct them.

Teaching Tips

- Use the STRATEGY Strategy (*see* Chapter 2, p. 16) to teach.
- Model how to use this strategy and the DEFENDS Planning Sheet.
- Have a two- to three-minute conference with students to review the planning sheet before they write their position papers.
- Use this strategy in all content areas that require position papers.

Putting Theory Into Practice

In the first step—**Decide** *on exact position*—students write down their positions. This writing step, as well as the next two writing steps, may be done on the DEFENDS Planning Sheet or students may be cued to write down their positions on notebook paper.

In the second step—**Examine** *the reasons for the position*—students write down two reasons and three details for each reason. This requirement adds length to what could otherwise be a short position paper. Again, this step can be done on the DEFENDS Planning Sheet or notebook paper.

The third step—**F**orm *a list of points that explain each reason*—requires students to sequence the reasons and details. This can be done after they have gotten their ideas down on paper.

The fourth step—**E**xpose *your position in the first sentence*—has students use their notes to write an initial draft of their position papers.

Next, students **N**ote *each reason and supporting point in their papers.* Again, they would use their planning notes.

The final sentence has students **D**rive *home the position*, followed by the last step, **S**earch *for errors and correct them.*

DEFENDS Planning Sheet

Decide on exact position. _____

_____

Examine the reasons for the position.

    Reason 1._____

        Detail 1. _____

        Detail 2. _____

        Detail 3. _____

    Reason 2. _____

        Detail 1._____

        Detail 2. _____

        Detail 3. _____

Form a list of points that explain each reason.

_____

_____

_____

_____

_____

_____

Now, begin writing a draft of the position paper using the following steps:

    Expose your position in the first sentence.

    Note each reason and supporting points.

    Drive home the position in the last sentence.

Edit the first draft using the last step:

    Search for errors and correct them.

PLEASE

Who: Marshall Welch

What: PLEASE

Where: Welch, M. (1992). The PLEASE strategy: A metacognitive learning strategy for improving the paragraph writing of students with mild learning disabilities. *Learning Disability Quarterly, 15*, 119–128.

When: Students need to write a paragraph.

Why: Students are often required to demonstrate understanding and mastery of different areas of content through written compositions. Many students find written expression difficult because they have poor planning and organizational skills.

How: PLEASE is a strategy for writing a paragraph. It was developed to address problems related to prewriting planning, composition, and paragraph revision. To use it, students need to follow these steps:

P = **P**ick a topic, an audience, and a format (e.g., compare and contrast).

L = **L**ist your ideas about the topic.

E = **E**valuate your list.

A = **A**ctivate the paragraph with a topic sentence.

S = **S**upply supporting sentences.

E = **E**nd with a concluding sentence and **E**valuate your work.

Teaching Tips

- Model all strategy steps for students (i.e., go through the steps aloud and provide literal examples as students listen).
- Have students memorize and rehearse the activities related to each strategy step.
- Use "controlled practice" (i.e., simulate assignments and use of the strategy steps), and provide supportive and corrective feedback until students demonstrate mastery.
- Use visual metaphors to illustrate parts of a paragraph. For example, compare a paragraph to parts of a sandwich: the top slice of bread is a topic sentence, the meat is the main idea, condiments are supporting details, and the bottom slice of bread is a concluding sentence.

Reportive Essay

Who: Bernice Wong, Roderick Wong, Deanna Darlington, and Wayne Jones

What: Reportive Essay (planning strategy)

Where: Wong, B., Wong, R., Darlington, D., & Jones, W. (1991). Interactive teaching: An effective way to teach revision skills to adolescents with learning disabilities. *Learning Disabilities Research and Practice, 6,* 117–127.

When: Students are writing essays.

Why: Often, students need a strategy to teach the planning stage of writing. This strategy teaches students to write about events in detail.

How: 1. Search long-term memory to retrieve events.

        2. Mentally relive the event fully through auditory and visual imageries.

        3. Reactivate all of the associated emotions.

Teaching Tips

- Teach students the importance of planning before they write.
- Model how to use this strategy.
- Prompt reluctant writers by brainstorming events in their life.

Putting Theory Into Practice

The first step—*Search long-term memory to retrieve events*—may require prompting. A list of topics or questions could be written on the chalkboard. (For example, if the event "The Worst Day I Ever Had" has been chosen, students need to think about all of the bad days they have experienced. Then, they decide which day was the worst.)

Next, students *mentally relive the event fully through auditory and visual imageries.* All of the events that occurred on that day need to be relived; specifically, students need to recall what they heard and saw that made that day so awful. The more detail, the better. (Continuing with the example topic, a student once came to school wearing two different shoes. During third period, she also discovered a big splotch of dried egg yolk on her cheek, and it had been there since she left home that morning! She would recall laughter and stares from her classmates.)

Finally, students *reactivate all of the associated emotions.* (In the example situation, the student would remember her red-faced embarrassment as the teacher asked her in front of the whole class, "Do you know that you are wearing two different shoes?")

TREE

Who: Steve Graham and Karen R. Harris

What: TREE (a strategy for composing opinion essays)

Where: Graham, S. & Harris, K.R. (1989). Improving learning disabled students' skills at composing essays: Self-instructional strategy training. *Exceptional Children, 56,* 201–214.

When: Students need to write opinion essays.

Why: Some students need a strategy to teach them how to write an opinion essay.

How: Develop a **Topic** sentence.

          Note **Reasons** to support premise.

          Examine reasons.

          Note **Ending** for the paper.

Teaching Tips

- Use the STRATEGY Strategy (*see* Chapter 2, p. 16) to teach.
- Have students generate ideas for their essays prior to writing.
- Teach students the importance of planning before writing.
- Use the TREE Planning Sheet.

Putting Theory Into Practice

Have students complete the following planning sheet when writing opinion essays.

> Slaves led existances of long and ornery work. Spartacus led a slave revolt and later was in a movie about this. The Roman republic was bothered by intestinal wars.

TREE PLANNING SHEET

Topic sentence:

_____

_____

Supporting **Reasons**:

_____

_____

_____

_____

Examine the soundness of each reason by placing a check mark next to it if it supports the topic sentence.

Ending sentence:

_____

_____

CHAPTER 5

MATHEMATICS SKILLS STRATEGIES

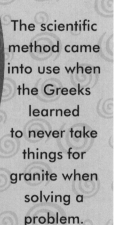

Arithmetic Problem Solving

Who: Jeannette E. Fleischner, Margaret B. Nuzum, and Eileen S. Marzola

What: Arithmetic Problem Solving

Where: Fleischner, J.E., Nuzum, M.B., & Marzola, E.S. (1987). Devising an instructional program to teach arithmetic problem-solving skills to students with learning disabilities. *Journal of Learning Disabilities, 20*, 214–217.

When: Students have difficulty solving mathematical word problems.

Why: Instruction in mathematical problem solving is usually restricted to textbook practices consisting of sequenced lists that illustrate what to do when solving problems (i.e., read, decide what to do, solve, and check your work). This kind of instruction is not very helpful for students who have limited resources for "deciding what to do."

How: 1. **READ:**   What is the question?

        2. **REREAD:**   What is the necessary information?

        3. **THINK:**   Putting together? (*Add*)

                Taking apart? (*Subtract*)

                Do I need all the information?

                Is it a two-step problem?

        4. **SOLVE:**   Write the equation.

        5. **CHECK:**   Recalculate.

                Label.

                Compare.

The scientific method came into use when the Greeks learned to never take things for granite when solving a problem.

Teaching Tips

- List the strategy steps on a card for each student and on a wall chart for easy access and review (*see* Content for Individual Prompt Cards and Wall Chart sample).
- Teach students to use the strategy to solve addition, subtraction, two-step problems, and problems with extraneous information.
- Allow students to solve problems orally or on paper.

  Limit the number of problems and have students show their work to ensure that they are completing each step of the strategy.

Putting Theory Into Practice

Students need to identify the information that is needed to solve or complete word problems. This means that they have to identify the question being asked, recognize unneeded information, and know when one or more mathematical operations are needed to solve the problem. Students also need task-specific information, such as the basic arithmetic concepts reflected in the problem (e.g., if items are being put together, addition is needed; if items are being taken away, subtraction is needed). Students must also be able to complete the needed arithmetic with complete accuracy; if any one of these components is missing, misunderstood, or mistaken, use of the Arithmetic Problem Solving Strategy will be compromised. Confirm students' understanding of each component before teaching them to use the strategy or before assuming they will be successful with it.

Content for Individual Prompt Cards and Wall Chart

ARITHMETIC PROBLEM SOLVING STRATEGY	
1. **READ**	What is the question?
2. **REREAD**	What is the necessary information?
3. **THINK**	Putting together? = Add
	Taking apart? = Subtract
	Is it a two-step problem?
4. **SOLVE**	Write the equation.
5. **CHECK**	Recalculate.
	Label.
	Compare.

(Fleischner, Nuzum, & Marzola, p. 216)

Division Facts

Who: John W. Lloyd, Nancy J. Saltzman, and James M. Kauffman

What: Division Facts

Where: Lloyd, J.W., Saltzman, N.J., & Kauffman, J.M. (1981). Predictable generalization in academic learning as a result of pre-skills and strategy training. *Learning Disability Quarterly, 4*, 203–216.

When: Students need help learning basic division facts.

Why: Multiplication and division are often among the most difficult basic skills for students with disabilities to master.

How: 1. Point to the divisor.

2. Count by the divisor until you get the number of the dividend.

3. Make hash marks while counting by.

4. Count the number of hash marks.

5. Write down the number of hash marks.

Teaching Tips

- Use the STRATEGY Strategy (*see* Chapter 2, p. 16) to teach.

Eight-Step Solving Strategy for Verbal Math Problems

Who: Marjorie Montague and Candace Bos

What: Eight-Step Solving Strategy for Verbal Math Problems

Where: Montague, M. & Bos, C. (1986). The effect of cognitive strategy training on verbal math problem solving performance of learning disabled adolescents. *Journal of Learning Disabilities, 19*, 26–33.

When: Solving mathematical word problems.

Why: Instruction in mathematical problem solving is usually restricted to textbook practices consisting of sequenced lists that illustrate what to do when solving problems (i.e., read, decide what to do, solve, and check your work). This kind of instruction is not very helpful for students who have limited resources for "deciding what to do."

How:
1. **Read** the problem aloud.

2. **Paraphrase** the problem aloud.

3. **Visualize.**

4. **State** the problem.

5. **Hypothesize.**

6. **Estimate.**

7. **Calculate.**

8. **Self-**check.

Teaching Tips

• Use the STRATEGY Strategy (*see* Chapter 2, p. 16) to teach.

• Students can read the problems to themselves.

• Limit the number of problems assigned (e.g., six to ten).

Math Problem Solving I

Who: Marjorie Montague

What: Math Problem Solving I

Where: Montague, M. (1992). The effects of cognitive and metacognitive strategy instruction on the mathematical problem solving of middle school students with learning disabilities. *Journal of Learning Disabilities, 25*, 230–248.

When: Students have difficulty solving mathematical word problems.

Why: Instruction in mathematical problem solving is usually restricted to textbook practices consisting of sequenced lists that illustrate what to do when solving problems (i.e., read, decide what to do, solve, and check your work). This kind of instruction is not very helpful for students who have limited resources for "deciding what to do."

How: 1. **Read** (for understanding).

    2. **Paraphrase** (your own words).

    3. **Visualize** (a picture or a diagram).

    4. **Hypothesize** (a plan to solve the problem).

    5. **Estimate** (predict the answer).

    6. **Compute** (do the arithmetic).

    7. **Check** (make sure everything is right).

Teaching Tips

- List the strategy steps on a card for each student and on a wall chart for easy access and review (*see* Content for Individual Prompt Cards and Wall Chart sample).
- Teach students to use the strategy to solve one-, two-, and three-step word problems.
- Allow students to solve problems orally or on paper.
- Limit the number of problems and have students show their work to ensure they are completing each step of the strategy (*see* Example Math Problem and Template for Students Using the Math Problem Solving I Strategy).

Putting Theory Into Practice

Montague (pp. 247–248) provided the following "dialogue" to illustrate portions of a scripted lesson used to teach the Math Problem Solving I Strategy:

Teacher: All right. Let's begin.

People who are good math problem solvers do several things in their heads when they solve problems. They use several processes. What is a process?

Student: (responds)

Teacher: A *process* is a thinking skill. What is a process?

Student: (repeats) A *process* is a thinking skill.

Teacher: Good problem solvers tell us they use the following seven processes when they solve math word problems. I have these processes on a card for you to keep and study at home and also on a big chart to use in class while you are learning the strategy. (Show [prompt] card and [wall] chart. Point to each step as you read, explain, or question.) First, good problem solvers **read** the problem for understanding. Why do you read math word problems?

Student: (repeats) I read for understanding.

Teacher: Then, good problem solvers **paraphrase** the problem. What does *paraphrase* mean?

Student: (responds)

Teacher: *Paraphrase* means to put the problem into your own words and remember the information. What does *paraphrase* mean?

Student: (repeats) *Paraphrase* means to put the problem into your own words and remember the information.

Teacher: The third process is **visualizing**. When people **visualize** word problems, they use objects to show the problem, or they draw a picture or a diagram of the problem on paper, or they make a picture in their head. How do people *visualize*?

Student: (repeats) They use objects to show the problem, or they draw a picture or a diagram of the problem on paper, or they make a picture in their head.

Teacher: Next, good problem solvers **hypothesize**. What does *hypothesize* mean?

Student: (responds)

Teacher:	*Hypothesize* means to set up a plan to solve the problem. What does *hypothesize* mean?
Student:	(repeats) *Hypothesize* means to set up a plan to solve the problem.
Teacher:	Then, people **estimate** the answer. What is *estimation*?
Student:	(responds)
Teacher:	*Estimation* means using the information in the problem to make a good *prediction* or to get a good idea about what the answer might be. What is *prediction*?
Student:	(responds)
Teacher:	People estimate, or *predict*, answers before they do the arithmetic. After they do the arithmetic and get the actual answer to the word problem, they compare their actual answer with the estimated answer. This helps them decide if the answer they found is right or if it is too big or too small. What is *estimating*?
Student:	(responds)
Teacher:	So after good problem solvers estimate their answers, they do the arithmetic. We call this **computing**. What is *computing*?
Student:	(repeats) *Computing* is doing the arithmetic.
Teacher:	Finally, good problem solvers check to make sure they have done everything right.

Content for Individual Prompt Cards and Wall Chart

MATH PROBLEM SOLVING I STRATEGY

1. **Read** (for understanding).
   - SAY: Read the problem. If I don't understand, read it again.
   - ASK: Have I read and understood the problem?
   - CHECK: For understanding as I solve the problem.

2. **Paraphrase** (your own words).
   - SAY: Underline the important information.
     Put the problem in my own words.
   - ASK: Have I underlined the important information?
     What is the question? What am I looking for?
   - CHECK: That the information goes with the question.

3. **Visualize** (a picture or a diagram).
   - SAY: Make a drawing or a diagram.
   - ASK: Does the picture fit the problem?
   - CHECK: The picture against the problem information.

4. **Hypothesize** (a plan to solve the problem).
   - SAY: Decide how many steps and operations are needed.
     Write the operation symbols (+, −, x, ÷).
   - ASK: If I do ... , what will I get?
     If I do ... , then what do I need to do next?
   - CHECK: That the plan makes sense.

5. **Estimate** (predict the answer).
   - SAY: Round the numbers, do the problem in my head,
     and write the estimate.
   - ASK: Did I round up or down?
     Did I write the estimate?
   - CHECK: That I used the important information.

6. **Compute** (do the arithmetic).
   - SAY: Do the operations in the right order.
   - ASK: How does my answer compare with my estimate?
     Does my answer make sense?
     Are the decimals or money signs in the right place?
   - CHECK: That all the operations were done in the right order.

7. **Check** (make sure everything is right).
   - SAY: Check the computation.
   - ASK: Have I checked every step?
     Have I checked the computation?
     Is my answer right?
   - CHECK: That everything is right. If not, go back.
     Then, ask for help if I need it.

(Montague, p. 234)

The following is an illustration of how a student might use the Math Problem Solving I Strategy.

Example Math Problem

1. **Read** (for understanding).	Roger had to pack videotapes 10 to a box. If he had 178 tapes of one kind and 121 of another kind, how many boxes would he need in order to pack them all and not mix the different types? (**a**) 13 boxes (**b**) 18 boxes (**c**) 30 boxes (**d**) 31 boxes
2. **Paraphrase** (your own words).	Putting 10 tapes to a box, how many boxes would it take to pack 178 tapes of one kind and 121 tapes of another kind?
3. **Visualize** (a picture or a diagram).	10 10 10 10 10 10 10 10 10 10 10 10 10 10 10 10 10 8 (18 boxes for 178 tapes) 10 10 10 10 10 10 10 10 10 10 10 10 10 1 (13 boxes for 131 tapes)
4. **Hypothesize** (a plan to solve the problem).	Decide how many boxes are needed for each set of tapes, and add the two answers together to determine the total number of boxes.
5. **Estimate** (predict the answer).	About 300 tapes, packed 10 to a box, would be about 30 boxes, if some of the tapes were mixed together.
6. **Compute** (do the arithmetic).	178 divided by 10 = 17.8 boxes (18 boxes) 121 divided by 10 = 12.1 boxes (13 boxes) 18 + 13 = 31 boxes
7. **Check** (make sure everything is right).	

Template for Students Using the Math Problem Solving I Strategy

1. **Read** (for understanding).	(Write the problem here.)
2. **Paraphrase** (your own words).	(Write the problem here in your own words.)
3. **Visualize** (a picture or a diagram).	(Draw a picture that solves the problem.)
4. **Hypothesize** (a plan to solve the problem).	(Write a plan that solves the problem.)
5. **Estimate** (predict the answer).	(Solve the problem using "round" numbers.)
6. **Compute** (do the arithmetic).	(Calculate an exact answer.)
7. **Check** (make sure everything is right).	(Check the math.)

Multiplication Facts

Who: John W. Lloyd, Nancy J. Saltzman, and James M. Kauffman

What: Multiplication Facts

Where: Lloyd, J.W., Saltzman, N.J., & Kauffman, J.M. (1981). Predictable generalization in academic learning as a result of pre-skills and strategy training. *Learning Disability Quarterly, 4*, 203–216.

When: Students need help learning basic multiplication facts.

Why: Multiplication and division are often among the most difficult basic skills for students with disabilities to master.

How: 1. Point to the number you can count by.

2. Make hash marks for the other numbers.

3. Count by the number, and point once for each hash mark.

4. Write down the last number you said.

Teaching Tips

• Use the STRATEGY Strategy (*see* Chapter 2, p. 16) to teach.

SOLVE

Who: Susan P. Miller and Cecil D. Mercer

What: SOLVE (completing math problems)

Where: Miller, S.P. & Mercer, C.D. (1993). Mnemonics: Enhancing math performance of students with learning difficulties. *Intervention in School and Clinic, 29*, 78–82.

When: Students need a mnemonic strategy to solve addition, subtraction, multiplication, and division problems.

Why: Some students need help in solving addition, subtraction, multiplication, and division problems. This strategy provides five steps to assist students.

How: S = **S**ee the sign.

O = **O**bserve and answer (if unable to answer, keep going).

L = **L**ook and draw.

V = **V**erify your answer.

E = **E**nter your answer.

Teaching Tips

- Use the STRATEGY Strategy (*see* Chapter 2, p. 16) to teach.
- Use highlighters to visually note mathematical signs (especially if using mixed practice).
- Use graph paper to line up problems.
- Provide a visual prompt to remind students to draw the problem.

Putting Theory Into Practice

The following describes how to use this strategy with the example problem:

$$\begin{array}{r} 4 \\ \times\,2 \\ \hline \end{array}$$

In the first step—**S**ee *the sign*—students look and see the multiplication sign.

In the second step—**O**bserve *and answer*—students stop at this step if they can answer the problem. If they are unable to answer, they keep going through the rest of the strategy steps.

In the third step—**Look** *and draw*—students look at the numbers and draw a picture to represent the problem:

$$4 \qquad \text{O O O O}$$
$$\underline{\times 2} \qquad \text{O O O O}$$

In the fourth step, students are reminded to **Verify** *your answer.* This is where they would double-check to see if their drawing was correct before counting up the circles to get the answer.

Finally, students are cued to **Enter** your answer:

$$4$$
$$\underline{\times 2}$$
$$\textbf{8}$$

Solving Simple Word Problems

Who: Lisa Pericola Case, Karen R. Harris, and Steve Graham

What: Solving Simple Word Problems

Where: Case, L.P., Harris, K.R., & Graham, S. (1992). Improving the mathematical problem-solving skills of students with learning disabilities: Self-regulated strategy development. *The Journal of Special Education, 26,* 1–19.

When: Students have difficulty solving mathematical word problems.

Why: Instruction in mathematical problem solving is usually restricted to textbook practices consisting of sequenced lists that illustrate what to do when solving problems (i.e., read, decide what to do, solve, and check your work). This kind of instruction is not very helpful for students who have limited resources for "deciding what to do."

How: 1. Read the problem out loud.

       2. Look for important words, and circle them.

       3. Draw pictures to help tell what is happening.

       4. Write down the math sentence.

       5. Write down the answer.

Teaching Tips

- List the strategy steps on a card for each student and on a wall chart for easy access and review (*see* Content for Individual Prompt Cards and Wall Chart sample).

- Teach students to use the strategy to solve addition and subtraction problems by concentrating on errors due to executing the wrong operation.

- Allow students to solve problems orally or on paper.

- Limit the number of problems and have students show their work to ensure that they are completing each step of the strategy.

- Students can read the problem silently.

- Highlight key words.

Putting Theory Into Practice

Discussion of the Problem-Solving Strategy. A small chart was used to introduce and discuss the problem-solving strategy. The steps of the strategy were to: (1) Read the problem out loud; (2) Look for important words, and circle them; (3) Draw pictures to help tell what is happening; (4) Write down the math sentence; and (5) Write down the answer. The instructor and student discussed why and how each step was used in solving word problems and discussed the importance of what we say to ourselves as we work and use the strategy. Students then generated and recorded on a small chart examples of things they could say to themselves to help find cue words or phrases in word problems.

Modeling of the Strategy and Self-Instructions. The student laid out the chart containing the strategy steps and the chart containing the self-generated instructions; the instructor modeled the use of the strategy while "thinking aloud." While modeling the strategy, the instructor used the following types of self-instructions to guide and direct behavior:

- Problem definition (e.g., "What is it I have to do?");
- Planning (e.g., "How can I solve this problem? ... By looking for important words.");
- Strategy use (e.g., "The five-step strategy will help me look for important words.");
- Self-evaluation (e.g., "How am I doing? Does this make sense?"); and
- Self-reinforcement (e.g., "I did a nice job; I got it right.").

Following modeling, the instructor and student discussed what the instructor said to help her do "good work" and use the strategy. The student then generated and recorded on the previously developed self-instruction chart other examples of things to say to oneself; the instructor made sure at least one statement in each of the five categories was included. It was stressed that self-statements did not always have to be verbalized aloud; once the student learned to use them, they could be thought "in your head or whispered to oneself." The strategy chart and self-instruction chart were kept in the student's mathematics folder.

Mastery of the Strategy Steps. The student rehearsed the problem-solving strategy until all five steps were memorized. Paraphrasing was allowed as long as meaning remained intact. The student's recall of the steps was assessed and practiced (as necessary) during subsequent sessions.

Collaborative Practice of the Strategy and Self-Instructions. The instructor and student collaboratively used the strategy to solve word problems. The strategy chart and the student-generated self-instruction list initially were available as prompts, but gradually were withdrawn as they were no longer needed. Similarly, the instructor provided the student with whatever assistance (including corrective feedback and positive reinforcement) was initially needed to use the strategy and self-instructions correctly; these supports also were withdrawn when no longer needed. The student was encouraged to use covert speech once mastery of the strategy and self-instructions was apparent.

Independent Performance. The student was directed to independently use the strategy and self-instructions to solve word problems. Together, the student and instructor recorded on the graph the number of items answered correctly. Once the student met the criterion of six of seven items correct, instruction for this phase was ended.

Generalization and Maintenance Components. Throughout the instructional sessions, students were reminded to use the strategy and self-instructions in their classrooms and asked to share occurrences of doing so with the instructor. The students also were encouraged to take their mathematics folders to their classroom and review or refer to them when appropriate. Students were further encouraged to talk to their teachers about the strategy and were required to have the special education teacher initial graphs during instruction. Finally, at the end of each lesson, the instructor and student discussed appropriate times to use the strategy.
(Case, Harris, & Graham, pp. 6–7)

Content for Individual Prompt Cards and Wall Chart

SOLVING SIMPLE WORD PROBLEMS STRATEGY

- 1. Read the problem out loud.

- 2. Look for important words, and circle them.

- 3. Draw pictures to help tell what is happening.

- 4. Write down the math sentence.

- 5. Write down the answer.

(Case, Harris, & Graham, p. 5)

Solving Word Problems

Who: Joan Karrison and Margaret K. Carroll

What: Solving Word Problems

Where: Karrison, J. & Carroll, M.K. (1991). Solving word problems. *Teaching Exceptional Children, 23* (4), 55–56.

When: Students need a strategy to solve word problems.

Why: Often, students need a simple, step-by-step strategy to solve word problems.

How: 1. Read the problem.

    2. <u>Underline</u> or **highlight** key words, sentences, or questions.

    3. Decide what sign to use.

    4. Set up the problem.

    5. Solve the problem.

Teaching Tips

- Use the STRATEGY Strategy (*see* Chapter 2, p. 16) to teach.
- Limit the number of word problems.
- Have students make a cue card of the strategy steps and place it in their math notebooks.
- Use removable highlighting tape to highlight in textbooks.
- Use highlighters on worksheets or other teacher-made materials.

Putting Theory Into Practice

In the first step, students **read the problem**:

Problem: Janice has a paper route. She delivers papers to 88 customers every day. Janice must also collect money from her customers each week. On Saturday, she collected money from 43 customers. How many customers must Janice collect money from on Sunday?

The second step tells students to <u>**underline**</u> or *highlight* **key words, sentences, or questions**:

Problem: Janice has a paper route. She delivers papers to <u>**88 customers**</u> every day. Janice must also collect money from her customers

each week. On Saturday, <u>she collected money from 43 customers.</u>
<u>How many customers must Janice collect money from on</u>
<u>Sunday</u>?

The third step is **decide what sign to use**. Students ask themselves if they need to add, subtract, multiply, or divide.

The fourth step has students **set up the problem**:

Subtract: 88
               <u>-43</u>

In the last step, students **solve the problem**:

88
<u>-43</u>
45

STAR

Who: Paula Maccini and Charles Hughes

What: STAR (for algebra word problems)

Where: Maccini, P. & Hughes, C.A. (2000). Effects of a problem-solving strategy on the introductory algebra performance of secondary students with learning disabilities. *Learning Disabilities Research & Practice, 15* (1), 10–21.

When: Students need a strategy to solve algebra word problems using concrete, semi-concrete, and abstract applications.

Why: Some students have difficulty solving algebra problems.

How: S = <u>S</u>earch the word problem:

1. Read the problem carefully.

2. Ask yourself questions:

   "What facts do I know?"

   "What do I need to find?"

3. Write down the facts.

T = <u>T</u>ranslate the words into an equation in picture form:

1. Choose a variable.

2. Identify the operation(s).

3. (a). Represent the problem with the Algebra Lab Gear (concrete application).

   (b). Draw a picture of the representation (semi-concrete application).

   (c). Write an algebraic equation (abstract application).

A = <u>A</u>nswer the problem:

Addition	Subtraction	Multiplication/ Division
Same signs: Add the numbers and keep the sign. **Different signs:** Find the difference of the numbers and keep the sign of the number farthest from zero.	Add the opposite of the second term.	**Same signs:** + **Different signs:** –

R = <u>R</u>eview the solution:

1. Reread the problem.

2. Ask yourself questions:

   "Does the answer make sense?"

   "Why?"

3. Check the answer.

Teaching Tips

- Use the STRATEGY Strategy (*see* Chapter 2, p. 16) to teach.
- Use highlighters to visually mark key information.
- Use Algebra Lab Gear or other materials in your classroom to demonstrate the concrete application. Also, allow students to use the materials to solve problems in the beginning stages of instruction.
- Teach students how to draw pictures to represent the semi-concrete applications.
- Require drawings as part of the math assignment.
- Transition students into using the abstract application.
- Teach students how to check their answers.

- Put sample problems and their answer sequences on a sheet for students to put in their notebooks as a reference.
- Write the steps on a cue card (index card or bookmark) and use to help solve problems.
- Put steps on a bulletin board.
- Have students solve problems orally or on paper.
- Limit the number of assigned problems, and have students show their work to ensure that they are completing each step of the strategy.

Putting Theory Into Practice

The following is an example of how to use the STAR Strategy with a word problem:

In Boone, North Carolina, the temperature on Wednesday morning was $-2°$ F. The temperature rose by $9°$ F by the afternoon. What was the temperature in the afternoon?

S = **S**earch the word problem:

1. Read the problem carefully.

2. Ask yourself questions:

    "What facts do I know?"

    "What do I need to find?"

    Wednesday temperature was −2 and it rose by 9.

    What was the temperature in the afternoon?

3. Write down the facts:

    Wednesday temperature was −2 and it rose by 9.

T = **T**ranslate the words into an equation in picture form:

1. Choose a variable −2 and 9.

2. Identify the operation(s):
    negative plus a positive

3. (a). Represent the problem with the Algebra Lab Gear (concrete application):

(Use algebra tiles or pieces of construction paper.)

For each of the groupings shown above, use different color tiles (e.g., red and blue).

Take the negative two tiles (red) and lay them over top of their counterparts in the positive group (blue).

By counting the remaining blue tiles, you will have the answer.

(b). Draw a picture of the representation (semi-concrete application):

OO   OOOOOOOOO (cancel opposites –2 +2)

-2º F   + 9º F = + 7º F

(c). Write an algebraic equation (abstract application):

-2º F + (+ 9º F) = x

Find the difference of the numbers:

+ 7º F = x

A = **Answer** the problem.

R = **Review** the solution:

1. Reread the problem.

2. Ask yourself questions:

    "Does the answer make sense?"

    "Why?"

3. Check the answer.

Subtraction Using the "4Bs" Mnemonic Strategy

Who: Alan R. Frank and Dianne Brown

What: Subtraction Using the "4Bs" Mnemonic Strategy (also use with addition)

Where: Frank, A.R. & Brown, D. (1992). Self-monitoring strategies in arithmetic. *Teaching Exceptional Children, 24*(2), 52–53.

When: Teaching students how to subtract.

Why: Some students have difficulty solving subtraction and addition problems.

How: **Begin**? In the 1s column.

Bigger? Which number is bigger?

Borrow? If bottom number is bigger, I must borrow.

Basic Facts? Remember them. (Use Touch Math, if needed.)

Teaching Tips

- Use the STRATEGY Strategy (*see* Chapter 2, p. 16) to teach.
- Teach students how to use Touch Math.
- Limit the number of problems to ten.
- Begin teaching the strategy using problems set up with cues (*see* Subtraction Worksheet for the "4Bs").
- After students become proficient in solving problems, fade the cues on the worksheet.

Putting Theory Into Practice

The "4Bs" in this mnemonic strategy help a student to remember the key word in each of the four steps: **Begin**, **Bigger**, **Borrow**, and **Basic** Facts. (Frank & Brown, p. 53) The Subtraction Worksheet for the "4Bs" includes a checklist with a mnemonic device above each problem.

This worksheet is for a student who is just learning the self-monitoring procedure for subtraction problems that may or may not require regrouping. The student begins the first problem by looking at the first ["B"] step in the list of directions at the top of the page, which prompts the selection of the 1s column as the correct starting place. After this column has been identified, the student places a check mark on the line next to the word **Begin**, above the 1s column. (The student checks next to **Begin** only once to indicate the he or she has started the problem in the correct column. Thus, only one line is provided.)

Next, the student refers to the second ["B"] step at the top of the page, which prompts him or her to determine which numeral in the 1s column is [bigger]. The student places a check mark on the line next to the word **Bigger** above the 1s column. When all steps required in the 1s column have been completed and checked off, the student then moves to the 10s and 100s columns, completing each step and checking it off in sequential order.

Using the "4Bs" with addition problems:

An analysis of the task of solving addition problems reveals that four critical steps are involved: (1) Start[ing] in the ones column; (2) Adding together the numerals in each column; (3) Determining whether or not regrouping is necessary; and (4) Checking to see whether or not the correct numeral has been carried to the next column when regrouping is necessary. The acronym SASH can be used as a mnemonic strategy to help students remember the steps:

- **Start** in the 1s column.
- **Add** the numerals together.
- **Should** I carry a numeral?
- **Have** I carried the correct numeral?

(Frank & Brown, p. 53)

SUBTRACTION WORKSHEET FOR THE "4BS"

Name _____

Date _____

Directions: SUBTRACT remembering the **4Bs**:

Begin?	In the first column.
Bigger?	Which number is bigger?
Borrow?	If bottom number is bigger, I must borrow.
Basic Facts?	Remember them.

_ **Begin**
___ **Bigger**
___ **Borrow**
___ **Basic** Facts

```
  8 5 3
- 3 8 8
```

_ **Begin**
___ **Bigger**
___ **Borrow**
___ **Basic** Facts

```
  9 2 4
-   1 7
```

_ **Begin**
___ **Bigger**
___ **Borrow**
___ **Basic** Facts

```
  6 6
- 2 4
```

_ **Begin**
___ **Bigger**
___ **Borrow**
___ **Basic** Facts

```
  2 3 6
-     9
```

_ **Begin**
___ **Bigger**
___ **Borrow**
___ **Basic** Facts

```
  4 7
- 3 5
```

_ **Begin**
___ **Bigger**
___ **Borrow**
___ **Basic** Facts

```
  5 3 5
- 3 3 8
```

_ **Begin**
___ **Bigger**
___ **Borrow**
___ **Basic** Facts

```
  6 7 9
- 3 5 9
```

_ **Begin**
___ **Bigger**
___ **Borrow**
___ **Basic** Facts

```
  2 0 6
-   8 3
```

_ **Begin**
___ **Bigger**
___ **Borrow**
___ **Basic** Facts

```
  7 3 1
- 3 5 1
```

Visual Prompt Strategy

Who: Spencer J. Salend and Elaine Hofstetter

What: Visual Prompt Strategy (for solving mathematical word problems)

Where: Salend, S.J. & Hofstetter, E. (1996). Adapting a problem-solving approach to teaching mathematics to students with mild disabilities. *Intervention in School and Clinic, 31*, 209–217.

When: Students are having difficulty solving mathematical word problems and a visual prompt would help.

Why: To teach students a visual strategy to assist them when solving any type of word problem.

How:
    1. Read the problem.

    2. Underline [or highlight] the important information.

    3. Cross out any information that is not needed.

    4. What type of problem is it?

    5. What operations do you need to use?

Teaching Tips

- Use the STRATEGY Strategy (*see* Chapter 2, p. 16) to teach.
- Students should be taught to use this strategy to solve one-, two-, and three-step word problems.
- Use a highlighter (if preferred) instead of underlining the important information.
- Use graph paper to line up problems.

Putting Theory Into Practice

Here is an example of how to use this strategy to solve simple word problems. The first step is **read the problem**:

Problem: Four friends have decided they want to go to the movies on Saturday. Tickets are $2.75 for students. One of the friends, Keith, had a birthday and just turned 18. Altogether they have $8.40. How much more do they need?

The second step is <u>**underline**</u> **[or highlight] the important information**:

Problem: Four friends have decided they want to go to the movies on Saturday. <u>Tickets are $2.75</u> for students. One of the friends, Keith, had a birthday and just turned 18. Altogether <u>they have $8.40. How much more do they need?</u>

Charles V
spent
most
of his
reign
aging.

The third step is **cross out any information that is not needed**. The following sentence is the information that is not needed and would be crossed out:

One of the friends, Keith, had a birthday and just turned 18.

The fourth step is where students decide **what type of problem is it**?

This problem is a two-step word problem.

Next, students decide **what type of operations do you need to use**?

Add, subtract, multiply, or divide?

Now, students are ready to solve the word problem.

CHAPTER 6

STUDY SKILLS STRATEGIES

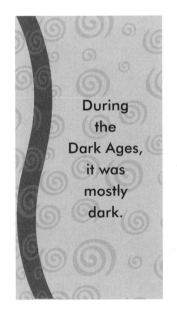

During the Dark Ages, it was mostly dark.

3Cs

Who: Brad W. Baxendell

What: 3Cs (use of graphic organizers)

Where: Baxendell, B.W. (2003). Consistent, coherent, creative: The 3Cs of graphic organizers. *Teaching Exceptional Children, 35*(3), 46–53.

When: Students with learning problems are expected to master the same rigorous content as their peers without learning problems.

Why: To assist students in understanding, organizing, and recalling important concepts and information.

How: A graphic organizer is a way of structuring information or arranging important parts of a problem, process, or topic into a pattern, using labels to reflect structure. **Consistent**, **coherent**, and **creative** (3Cs) practices facilitate the use of graphic organizers during instruction and practice.

<u>C</u>onsistent:

• Use a standard set of graphic organizers (*see* the four types of graphic organizers).

    • Establish a routine for using graphic organizers.

<u>C</u>oherent:

    • Use labels for relations between concepts in graphic organizers.

    • Limit the number of concepts or relations covered in graphic organizers.

    • Minimize distractions when using graphic organizers.

<u>C</u>reative:

    • Assign homework and test review for practice using graphic organizers.

    • Do not limit the use of graphic organizers.

- Structure cooperative groups and pairs when using graphic organizers.

- Add illustrations to graphic organizers.

Teaching Tips

- Use a consistent type of graphic organizer (e.g., cause-effect) for similar types of instruction (e.g., reading fiction and nonfiction, preparing written compositions, doing science experiments).

- Encourage grade-level and schoolwide use of graphic organizers to establish consistency.

- Use clear, coherent designs that are free of distracting information.

- Use labels for ideas and concepts on graphic organizers to assure coherence.

- Encourage classroom and home use of graphic organizers to foster creativity.

- Use creative variations of graphic organizers for different types of learning experiences (e.g., cooperative groups or learning pairs).

Putting Theory Into Practice

Baxendell (pp. 49–51) suggests using the following four types of graphic organizers:

1. Cause-Effect Graphic Organizer

Demonstrates relations between single or multiple cause(s) and effect(s).

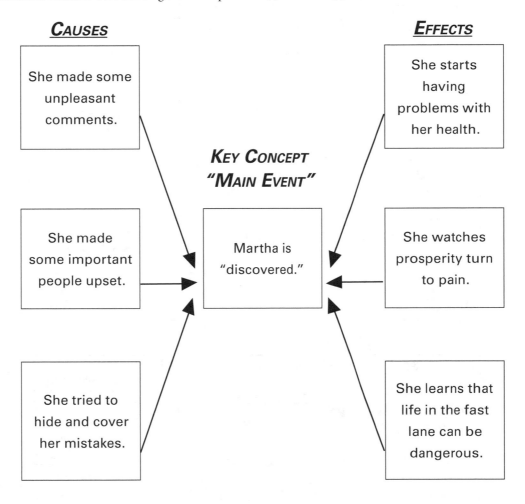

2. Sequence Chart Graphic Organizer

Illustrates chain of events, actions, or relations in solving a problem.

IDENTIFY PROBLEM

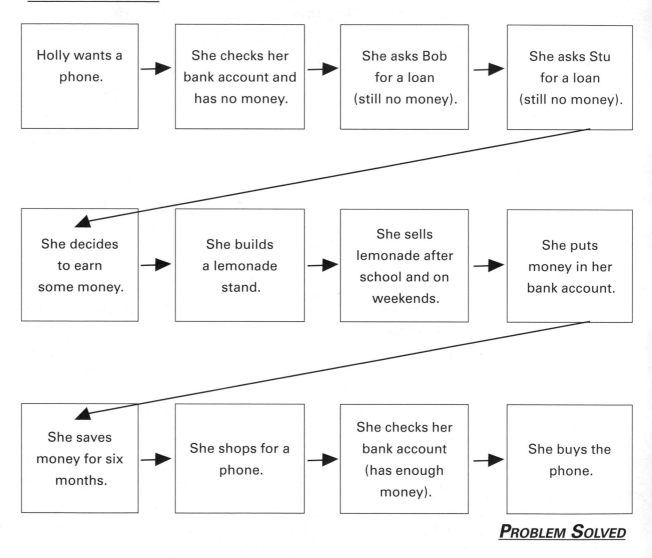

Holly wants a phone. → She checks her bank account and has no money. → She asks Bob for a loan (still no money). → She asks Stu for a loan (still no money).

She decides to earn some money. → She builds a lemonade stand. → She sells lemonade after school and on weekends. → She puts money in her bank account.

She saves money for six months. → She shops for a phone. → She checks her bank account (has enough money). → She buys the phone.

PROBLEM SOLVED

3. Main Idea-and-Details Graphic Organizer

Illustrates important parts of a topic.

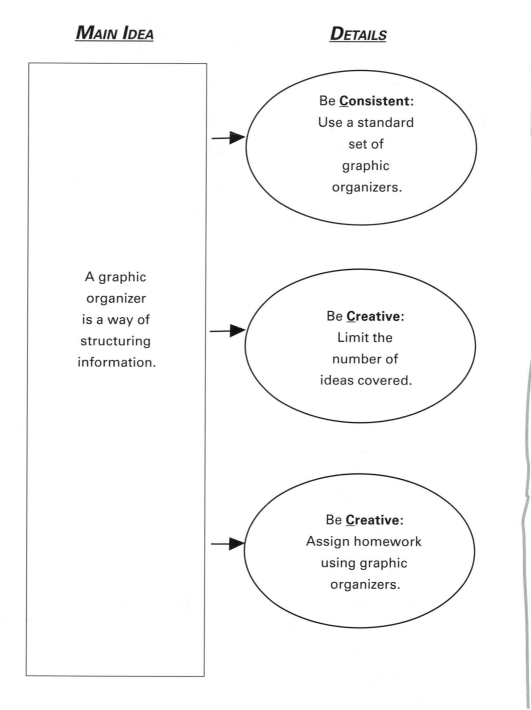

4. Venn Diagram

Illustrates similarities and differences between ideas, concepts, people, places, and things.

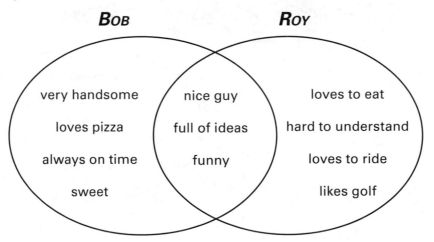

BOB   **ROY**

very handsome   nice guy   loves to eat

loves pizza   full of ideas hard to understand

always on time   funny   loves to ride

sweet   likes golf

FLIP

Who:	Jean S. Schumm and Charles T. Mangrum II
What:	FLIP
Where:	Schumm, J.S. & Mangrum II, C.T. (1991). FLIP: A framework for content area reading. *Journal of Reading, 35*(2), 120–124.
When:	Students need help reading in the content areas.
Why:	This strategy is designed to help middle and high school students examine reading assignments and design an action plan.
How:	**F** = <u>F</u>riendliness: How friendly is my reading assignment?
	L = <u>L</u>anguage: How difficult is the language in my reading assignment?
	I = <u>I</u>nterest: How interesting is my reading assignment?
	P = <u>P</u>rior knowledge: What do I already know about the material covered in my reading assignment?

Teaching Tips

- Use FLIP with any reading assignment.
- Make FLIP cue cards or bookmarks for students.
- Put posters of FLIP steps in general education classrooms.
- Have students decide on their purpose for reading.
- Have students think about the needed reading rate for the assignment (i.e., **fast** for familiar material, **medium** for material that may need careful thought, or **slow** for material that is unfamiliar and may require rereading of passages).

Putting Theory Into Practice

F(riendliness): Students examine their [reading] assignment to locate friendly text features. Here is a sample of friendly text features (Schumm & Mangrum, pp. 121–122):

Table of Contents	Index	Glossary
Chapter introduction	Headings	Subheadings
Margin notes	Study questions	Chapter summary
Key terms highlighted	Graphs	Charts
Pictures	Signal words	List of key facts

L(anguage): With FLIP, students skim the [reading] assignment to see how many new terms are introduced. Then, they read three random paragraphs to get the feel for the vocabulary level and the number of long, complicated sentences. Using this quick gauge, they rate the language from 1 to 5, keeping in mind that 5 means there are no new words and mostly clear sentences and 1 means there are many new words and complicated sentences.

I(nterest): Here, students read the assignment's title, introduction, headings and subheadings, and summary, and examine its pictures and graphics.

P(rior knowledge): The quick survey completed during the "I" step should let readers determine if they have prior knowledge of the assignment's subject matter. Overall, this reading assignment appears to be at:

    _____ A comfortable reading level for me.

    _____ A somewhat comfortable reading level for me.

    _____ An uncomfortable reading level for me.

IQ WHO

Who: Edwin S. Ellis and B. Keith Lenz

What: IQ WHO

Where: Ellis, E.S. & Lenz, B.K. (1987). A component analysis of effective learning strategies for LD students. *Learning Disabilities Focus, 2,* 94–107.

When: Students with disabilities often experience difficulties in locating information in textbook chapters in content areas. for many, these problems are related to inefficient study skills.

Why: Students with disabilities often experience difficulties in locating information in textbook chapters in content areas. For many, these problems are related to inefficient study skills.

How: I = <u>I</u>llustrations interpreted.

        Q = <u>Q</u>uestions at the end of the chapter read and paraphrased.

        W= <u>W</u>ords in italics defined.

        H = <u>H</u>eadings: For each, do RASPN:

            R = <u>R</u>ead a heading.

            A = <u>As</u>k self a question based on heading topic.

            S = <u>S</u>can for the answer.

            P = <u>P</u>ut answer in own words.

            N= <u>N</u>ote important information.

        O = <u>O</u>ther clues that textbook employs are identified and used.

Teaching Tips

- Describe the strategy steps to students, including where, when, why, and how the strategy can be used.
- Model all strategy steps for students (e.g., go through each step while speaking aloud as students listen).
- Have students memorize and rehearse the activities related to each strategy step.
- Use "controlled practice" (e.g., simulate assignments and use of the strategy steps), and provide supportive and corrective feedback until students demonstrate mastery.

Putting Theory Into Practice

Use the IQ WHO Checklist (*see* below) as students read through a chapter. In the initial strategy instruction, the teacher may want to read through the chapter and model how to use IQ WHO. This strategy may be useful in a co-teach setting; if presented to a whole class, it may help all students in the classroom, not just students with learning disabilities. To help motivate students, count this activity as an assignment for the chapter.

IQ WHO CHECKLIST

___ **I** = **I**llustrations interpreted.

___ **Q** = **Q**uestions at the end of the chapter read and paraphrased.

    1. _____

    2. _____

    3. _____

    4. _____

    5. _____

___ **W** = **W**ords in italics defined.

    (Write the definitions in your notebook. Put page numbers for future reference and examples.)

___ **H** = **H**eadings: For each, do RASPN:

    ___ **R** = **R**ead a heading.

    ___ **A** = **A**sk self a question based on heading topic.

    ___ **S** = **S**can for the answer.

    ___ **P** = **P**ut answer in own words.

    ___ **N** = **N**ote important information.

        (Use RASPN to take notes from the chapter.)

___ **O** = **O**ther clues that textbook employs are identified and used.

Keywords

Who: Heather Zrebiec Uberti, Thomas E. Scruggs, and Margo A. Mastropieri

What: Keywords

Where: Uberti, H.Z., Scruggs, T.E., & Mastropieri, M.A. (2003). Keywords make the difference! Mnemonic instruction in inclusive classrooms. *Teaching Exceptional Children, 35*(3), 56–61.

When: Students in inclusive classrooms are challenged with learning and retaining general education content. This strategy will help them learn and remember relevant vocabulary.

Why: To improve verbal learning and memory.

How: This strategy creates a concrete, similar-sounding alternative for an unfamiliar word that is being learned. It involves several steps:

1. Examine reading materials and textbooks for important and challenging vocabulary words.

2. Make a list of important and challenging words and their definitions.

3. Recode important and challenging words to keywords or cue words (e.g., *daze* sounds like *maze*).

4. Create a visual representation of keyword and meaning to be remembered. For example:

   A good keyword for the vocabulary word *fjord* could be board, since it sounds like *fjord* and is easy to picture. The next step is to show the keyword with the definition. In this case, a *board* floating on the water between two cliffs could be pictured. When students hear the vocabulary word (*fjord*), they should first think of the keyword (*board*), then think about the keyword picture (a board floating on the water between two cliffs), remember what was happening in the keyword picture, and then remember the definition of the vocabulary word (a *fjord* is "a body of water between steep slopes").

Teaching Tips

• Use the Keywords Strategy to improve vocabulary in content-area subjects (e.g., Science, Social Studies, foreign languages).

• Have students learn the keyword first and then the picture that goes with it.

• Help students remember the picture of the keyword and the definition together.

• Tell students to think of the keyword and what is represented in the picture before trying to remember the definition.

Putting Theory Into Practice

Here is a sample script and graphic to use when teaching the Keywords Strategy:

Teacher: Here is a good way to remember the definition of the vocabulary word *daze*. When you hear the word *daze*, think of the keyword *maze*. *Daze* sounds like *maze*, and you can easily think of a picture for it. What is the keyword for the vocabulary word *daze*? *Maze*. That's right!

Now, when you think of *maze*, think of a picture of a maze and a man in a state of confusion about which way to go. When you are asked to define *daze*, think of the keyword that sounds like *daze*. What is it? Great! It's *maze*!

Now, think about the picture of the maze and what is happening in it. Right, the man is in a state of confusion. That should help you remember the definition for *daze*. What is the definition of *daze*? Super! . . . "a state of confusion."

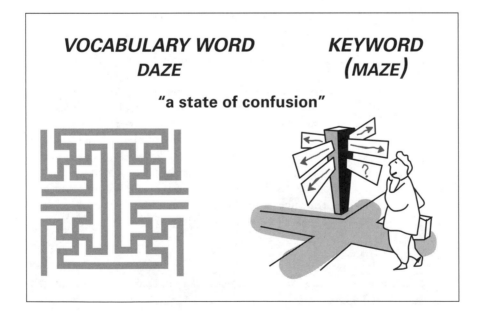

VOCABULARY WORD
DAZE

KEYWORD
(MAZE)

"a state of confusion"

PASS Executive Strategy

Who: Edwin S. Ellis

What: PASS Executive Strategy (for writing and reading)

Where: Ellis, E.S. (1994). Integrating writing strategy instruction with content-area instruction: Part 1—Orienting students to organizational devices. *Intervention in School and Clinic, 29*(3), 169–179.

When: Students need a strategy to assist them in listening, reading, or writing in any content area.

Why: Knowing how to study is a critical element for success at any grade level.

How: P = <u>P</u>review, review, and predict (*think ahead*).

A = <u>A</u>sk and answer questions (*think during*).

S = <u>S</u>ummarize.

S = <u>S</u>ynthesize (*think back*).

Teaching Tips

- Use with graphic organizers when presenting content.
- Have students **Preview**, *review, and predict* material to obtain a general sense of themes, concepts, and information reflected in headings and general organization of content presentation.
- Have students **Ask** *and answer questions* before reading to make sure they have identified a purpose or the purposes being emphasized in a passage or before listening to a content-area lecture with note-taking.
- Have students **Summarize** the information, possibly using a graphic organizer.
- Have students **Synthesize** the information that has been presented to them.

Putting Theory Into Practice

The following guide (Ellis, p. 220) shows how to use the PASS Executive Strategy for writing.

PASS EXECUTIVE STRATEGY FOR WRITING

P = **Preview**, review, and predict.
- Preview your knowledge, audience, and goals.
- Review main ideas/details to tell.
- Predict best order.

A = **Ask** and answer questions.

Topic-/reader-related questions:
- How can I activate the reader's knowledge in the first sentence?
- What background knowledge does the reader have that I can link this idea to?
- What else can I say? Have I left anything out?
- What would be a good example of what I mean?
- Does this make sense? Should I explain this idea more?

Problem-solving questions:
- Should I get more information from others?
- Where can I look up more information?
- Should I rephrase this to make it more clear?

S = **Summarize** the message in the last sentence.

S = **Synthesize** the information.

The following guide (Ellis, p. 225) shows how to use the PASS Executive Strategy for reading.

PASS EXECUTIVE STRATEGY FOR READING

P = Preview, review, and predict.

- Preview the text (title, headings, pictures, etc.).
- Review what you already know about this topic.
- Predict what you think the text will be about.

A = Ask and answer questions.

Topic-related questions:

- Who? What? When? Where? Why? How?
- How does this relate to what I already know?
- Is my prediction correct?
- How is this different from what I thought it was going to be about?

Problem-solving questions:

- Does this make sense?
- Is it important that it makes sense, or can I skip this part?
- Do I need to reread part of it? Can I visualize the information?
- Do I need to read it more slowly? Do I need to pay more attention?
- Should I get help?

S = Summarize

- Say what the short passage was about.

S = Synthesize

- Say how the passage fits in with what the whole thing is about.
- Say how what you learned fits with what you know.

PREP

Who: Edwin S. Ellis

What: PREP

Where: Ellis, E.S. (1993). Integrative strategy instruction: A potential model for teaching content area subjects to adolescents with learning disabilities. *Journal of Learning Disabilities, 26* (6), 358–383.

When: Students often need assistance in class preparation. This strategy will help students learn the content in classes.

Why: To assist students in preparing for class.

How: P = <u>P</u>repare materials:

   • Mark notes, study guide, and textbook.

   • Get notebook, study guide, pencil, and textbook ready for class.

R = <u>R</u>eview what you know:

   • Read notes, study guide, and textbook cues.

   • Relate cues to what you already know about the topic.

E = <u>E</u>stablish positive mind-set:

   • Tell yourself to learn.

   • Suppress put-downs of yourself.

   • Make a positive self-statement.

P = <u>P</u>inpoint goals:

   • Decide what you want to find out, and create questions.

   • Note participation goals.

Teaching Tips

• Teach students what parts of the strategy they need to do as homework (*see* PREP Checksheet).

• Send a copy of the strategy to parents. They can encourage the use of PREP at home.

• Ask parents to post the PREP Checksheet where their child does homework.

• Teach students to use a highlighter to mark notes.

• Use highlighting tape to mark key information in the textbook.

Putting Theory Into Practice

PREP Checksheet

Directions: Place a check mark next to each step when it is completed.

_____ **P** = **Prepare** materials:

_____ • Mark notes, study guide, and textbook.

_____ • Get notebook, study guide, pencil, and textbook ready for class.

_____ **R** = **Review** what you know:

_____ • Read notes, study guide, and textbook cues.

_____ • Relate cues to what you already know about the topic.

_____ **E** = **Establish** positive mind-set:

_____ • Tell yourself to learn: "I am read to study my science."

_____ • Suppress put-downs of yourself.

_____ • Make a positive self-statement. Say a positive affirmation such as, "I am doing a great job studying!"

_____ **P** = **Pinpoint** goals:

_____ • Decide what you want to find out, and create questions:

"I need to know _____

_____

_____

_____

_____ "

_____ Questions for what I need to know:

_____

_____

_____

_____ • Note participation goals:

Here are my goals:

1. _____

2. _____

3. _____

PREPARE

Who: Edwin S. Ellis and B. Keith Lenz.

What: PREPARE

Where: Ellis, E.S. & Lenz, B.K. (1987). A component analysis of effective learning strategies for LD students. *Learning Disabilities Focus, 2,* 97–101.

When: Students have problems preparing for class.

Why: Some students have difficulty establishing an effective locker-visit routine and deciding what they need for classes. Students often need assistance in getting their thoughts together at the beginning of class and reviewing information after class.

How: P = **P**lan locker visits.

R = **R**eflect on what you need and get.

E = **E**rase personal needs.

P = **P**SYC self up:

     P = **P**ause for attitude check.

     S = **S**ay a personal goal related to class.

     Y = **Y**oke in negative thoughts.

     C = **C**hallenge self to good performance.

A = **A**sk self where class has been and where class is going.

R = **R**eview notes and study guide.

E = **E**xplore meaning of teacher's introduction.

Teaching Tips

- Use STRATEGY Strategy (*see* Chapter 2, p. 16) to teach.
- Have students write personal goals for each class.
- Teach how to review notes and study guides.
- Teach a note-taking strategy.
- Brainstorm the best time for students to go to their lockers.

Putting Theory Into Practice

In the first step—**Plan** *locker visit*s—it is important to help students decide the best times to go to their lockers. It may not be feasible for them to go between each class.

Depending on the location of the locker, students may need to go to their locker just once in the morning to get the necessary books and materials for classes prior to lunch. After lunch, students may need to get all their books for afternoon classes and wait until the end of the school day to get their books for homework.

The second step—**Reflect** *on what you need and get*—would be done each time a student goes to his or her locker. Some students may need to make a list to help them get all of the necessary materials; other students may just need to use their assignment notebook or calendar to guide them.

The third step—**Erase** *personal need*s—includes not socializing in the hallways too much, not going to a vending machine instead of getting a textbook, etc. It is important to teach students how to manage their time between classes. Some students experience a lot of difficulty with this and, as a result, are often tardy for class.

The fourth step—**PSYC** *self up*—has students mentally prepare themselves for class. Again, this needs to be taught. Students do not know how to give themselves pep talks and think about how the teacher will respond to their attitudes when they walk into class.

The fifth step—**Ask** *self where class has been and where class is going*—occurs as soon as students sit down in class. This requires students to mentally begin preparing for the content about to be presented. This ties right into the sixth step: **Review** *notes and study guide.*

The last step—**Explore** *meaning of teacher's introduction*—requires students to start paying attention the moment class begins. This gets students in the right mind-set for the day's lesson.

PROJECT

Who: Charles A. Hughes, Kathy L. Ruhl, Jean B. Schumaker, and Donald D. Deshler

What: PROJECT (an assignment completion strategy)

Where: Hughes, C.A., Ruhl, K.L., Schumaker, J.B., & Deshler, D.D. (2002). Effects of instruction in an assignment completion strategy on the homework performance of students with learning disabilities in general education classes. *Learning Disabilities Research and Practice, 17,* 1–18.

When: Students, especially those with poor organizational skills and difficulties with task completion, need assistance in completing homework and other assignments.

Why: Homework is one of the common demands of schooling. In many school districts, policies have been established for amounts of homework assigned each week, and grades on assignments completed out of school are part of a teacher's overall assessment of a student's academic progress.

How: P = <u>P</u>repare your forms.

R = <u>R</u>ecord and ask.

O = <u>O</u>rganize:

<u>B</u>reak the assignment into parts.

<u>E</u>stimate the number of study sessions.

<u>S</u>chedule the sessions.

<u>T</u>ake your materials home.

J = <u>J</u>ump to it.

E = <u>E</u>ngage in the work.

C = <u>C</u>heck your work.

T = <u>T</u>urn in your work.

Teaching Tips

- Describe the strategy steps to students, including where, when, why, and how the strategy can be used.
- Model all strategy steps for students (e.g., go through each step while speaking aloud as students listen).

- Have students memorize and rehearse the activities related to each strategy step.
- Use "controlled practice" (e.g., simulate assignments and use of the strategy steps), and provide supportive and corrective feedback until students demonstrate mastery.

Putting Theory Into Practice

In the first step of the strategy—**P**repare *your forms*—students complete a two-month planning calendar with "special events" (e.g., birthdays, holidays, trips) to be considered when planning upcoming homework assignments (*see* Two-Month Planning Calendar sample). A weekly schedule, which blocks out times that are unavailable to do homework, is also completed (*see* Weekly Schedule sample).

The second step of the strategy—**R**ecord *and ask*—is engaged when students receive a homework assignment. Students quickly and accurately record the assignment on an assignment sheet (*see* Assignment Sheet sample), using abbreviations, such as SS = Social Studies and RPT = Report, to facilitate understanding of the assignment. Students also record the due date of the homework assignment on the Two-Month Planning Calendar and the Weekly Schedule, and ask any questions about parts of the assignment that may be unclear.

In the third step of the strategy—**O**rganize—students develop a BEST study schedule after all daily assignments have been given and prepare materials to take home to facilitate completion of any homework:

- First, students **B**reak *the assignment into parts* (e.g., book report = select a book, read the book, make notes, do a first draft, and do a final draft) and record the number of parts on the Assignment Sheet.
- Next, students **E**stimate *the number of study sessions* required to complete the assignment and record the number on the Assignment Sheet.
- Next, students **S**chedule the sessions on the Weekly Schedule planner, taking care to schedule sessions enough in advance to complete the assignment on time (*see* Sample Script below).
- Finally, students **T**ake materials home that are needed to complete the scheduled assignment(s).

Students use the next three PROJECT Strategy steps—**J**ump *to it*, **E**ngage *in the work*, and **C**heck *your work*—to overcome task avoidance and start working on an assignment; to complete the assignment and make note of any problems that may require assistance from parents, study buddies, or the teacher; and to evaluate the overall quality of their homework assignment.

The last step—<u>T</u>urn *in your work*—takes place after an assignment has been completed. Students put the completed work in a place where it can be easily found (e.g., in a folder in a backpack by the door). At school, students turn in the assignment and check it off their Two-Month Planning Calendar and Weekly Schedule.

Sample Script Segment for Teaching the **Schedule** *Sessions* Substep
During the Model Stage of Instruction

Teacher: "Next, I'll schedule the study sessions for the assignments I got today. I'll start with the ones due tomorrow because I want to make sure I have time to get my assignments for tomorrow done tonight. Let's see...what assignments are due tomorrow?" (Teacher checks the Monthly Planner and Assignment Sheets.)

"Hmm... I have a Math and a Spanish assignment due. I already estimated that Math will take one 30-minute session, and Spanish will take about two sessions. I add one plus two and see that I need to schedule three sessions tonight. I look at my Weekly Schedule and see that I have slots open between 4:30 P.M. and 6:00 P.M. I'll write 'Math' in one of the boxes and 'Spanish' in two of the boxes in that time slot." [Teacher writes subject names in the appropriate boxes.] "Then I'll have dinner, and the rest of the evening will be free."

(Hughes, Ruhl, Schumaker, & Deshler, 2002, p. 9)

Two-Month Planning Calendar

Sunday	Monday	Tuesday	Wednesday	Thursday	Friday	Saturday
						1
2	3	4 M/TEST	5	6	7	8
9	10	11	12 SS/RPT	13	14	15
16	17	18	19	20	21	22
23	24	25	26	27	28	1
2	3	4	5	6	7	8
9	10	11 BIO TEST	12	13	14	15
16	17	18	19	20	21	22
23	24	25	26	27	28	29
30	31					

Weekly Schedule

Date	1	2	3	4	5	6	7
Day	Saturday	Sunday	Monday	Tuesday	Wednesday	Thursday	Friday
Time							
6:30–3:30			School	School	School	School	School
3:30–4:00		OPEN					
4:00–6:00		OPEN	SS/RPT	SS/RPT	OPEN	OPEN	OPEN
6:00–6:30							
6:30–8:30		BIO	M/TEST	BIO	BIO	BIO	OPEN
8:30–9:00		OPEN	M/TEST	OPEN	OPEN	OPEN	OPEN
9:00–10:00		OPEN		OPEN	OPEN	OPEN	OPEN

Assignment Sheet

Subject			Due Date	Date Completed
BIO	*Read*	Chapter 7—Cells	April 7	April 6
	Answer	Chapter Study Questions		
Number of Parts	3			
Estimated Sessions	4			

PROVE

Who: David Scanlon

What: PROVE

Where: Scanlon, D. (2002). PROVE-ing what you know: Using a learning strategy in an inclusive environment. *Teaching Exceptional Children, 34*(4), 48–54.

When: Students need assistance stating what they know, explaining it, and defending their understanding; these skills typically are required in content-area classrooms.

Why: Many students have difficulties demonstrating what they know, or they are so unsure of what they know that their reply to a direct question from a teacher is, "I don't know."

How: P = **Present** the knowledge I will PROVE.

           R = **Reveal** information to support my knowledge.

           O = **Offer** evidence to support my knowledge.

           V = **Verify** my knowledge.

           E = **Express** my knowledge in a Summary Statement.

Teaching Tips

- Describe the strategy steps to students, including where, when, why, and how the strategy can be used.
- Model all strategy steps for students (e.g., go through each step while speaking aloud as students listen).
- Have students memorize and rehearse the activities related to each strategy step.
- Use "controlled practice" (e.g., simulate assignments and use of the strategy steps), and provide supportive and corrective feedback until students demonstrate mastery.

Putting Theory Into Practice

In the first step of the strategy—**Present** *the knowledge I will PROVE*—students identify a statement that expresses what is known or believed about a topic (e.g., "Dogs are vertebrates"). The statement serves as a cue for students in beginning to use the strategy (*see* PROVE Worksheet).

The second step of the strategy—**Reveal** *information to support my knowledge*—requires students to provide a reason or indication for why the initial proposition is true (e.g., "Dogs have backbones"). This step helps students demonstrate knowledge in ways other than rote memorization.

Once a rationale has been stated, students are asked to **Offer** *evidence to support my knowledge*. The evidence, explanation, or examples illustrate how the proposition is true (e.g., "A skeleton of a dog clearly shows a backbone, with ribs attached to it").

In the fourth step—**Verify** *my knowledge*—students will investigate literal sources of information to supplement their personal knowledge of the subject. Students may ask a teacher or a peer to confirm what they know. Students may also identify sources of knowledge (e.g., encyclopedias, legitimate Web sites) that will confirm a proposition.

In the final step—**Express** *my knowledge in a Summary Statement*—students account for what is known in a brief written paragraph. The summary includes evidence to support what is known.

PROVE WORKSHEET

Present the knowledge I will PROVE.

_____

_____

Reveal information to support my knowledge.

_____

_____

Offer evidence to support my knowledge.

_____

_____

Verify My Knowledge.

_____   _____

_____   _____

Source: _____   Source: _____

Express my knowledge in a Summary Statement.

_____

_____

_____

_____

Monks were assigned to monkeries, where they were supposed to live as nuns. Fryers were required to take a vow of pottery.

CHAPTER 7

SOCIAL SKILLS STRATEGIES

Dealing With Anger

Who: Ellen McGinnis, Lorrie Sauerbry, and Polly Nichols

What: Dealing With Anger

Where: McGinnis, E., Sauerbry, L., & Nichols, P. (1985). Skill-streaming: Teaching social skills to children with behavioral disorders. *Teaching Exceptional Children, 17*(3), 160–167.

When: Students need to learn how to control their behaviors and decide on how to react or respond to various situations.

Why: Educating children with behavior problems means more than simply teaching academic skills and setting limits on what they can and cannot do. These students also need to have direct instruction in interpersonal and social skills, such as dealing with anger.

How: Teach students to follow these steps when dealing with anger:

1. Stop and count to 10.

2. Think of your choices:

   a. Tell the person why you are angry.

   b. Walk away now.

   c. Do a relaxation exercise.

3. Act out your best choice.

Teaching Tips

- List the steps on a card for each student and on a wall chart for easy access and review.
- Teach students that these are ways to deal with their anger that will not make other people angry.

New things loamed on the horizon.

- Let students practice "choices" by asking you if they can leave the room, run an errand, or go outside for a few minutes.
- Teach students to use the strategy when they think that you, their parents, or their peers have not been fair to them or when they are having a "bad day . . . where everything seems to be going wrong."

I CAN

Who: David P. Swanson

What: I CAN (a personal commitment strategy)

Where: Swanson, D.P. (1992). I CAN. *Teaching Exceptional Children,4*(2), 22–26.

When: Students need motivation to complete their class assignments.

Why: Students often focus on what they *cannot* do, rather than on what they *can* do. This strategy uses the acronym I CAN to motivate students to complete daily assignments.

How:
I = **I**ndependence (work alone).

C = **C**ompletion (of work).

A = **A**ccuracy (reach a mastery level).

N = **N**eatness (write neatly).

Teaching Tips

- Write individual contracts with students (*see* I CAN Sample Contract).
- Review goals with students before and after lessons.
- Reward students for reaching target goals.
- Put a copy of the contract in the students' folders.
- To serve as a reminder, tape an index card that lists students' goals on their desks.

Putting Theory Into Practice

Use goals on the student's IEP to determine target areas for an I CAN Contract. Write the goals on the contract with the student (this can be done at or after the IEP meeting). The student can self-monitor his or her daily progress on a calendar or a chart. Use tally marks or stars to indicate which target behaviors were met on a daily basis.

Sample Contract for I CAN Sample Contract

Date: _____

I, _____ , am responsible for my behavior and I can work on the following skills:

<u>I</u>ndependence: I CAN work by myself for 20 minutes for 5 days in a row when I do seatwork.

<u>C</u>ompletion: CAN finish 8 out of 10 problems on my math a signment for 5 days in a row.

<u>A</u>ccuracy: I CAN maintain an 80% average on my reading assignments for 5 days in a row.

<u>N</u>eatness: I CAN write my spelling words neatly for 5 days in a row.

_____ will earn the following reward(s) when he/she meets his/her goals:

1. Have 20 minutes of free play on the computer.
2. Have 15 minutes of free time on a Friday.
3. Choose an item from the class store.

Signatures: _____ (Teacher)

_____ (Student)

Contract Completed Date:_____

Contract Revised Date _____

LISTEN

Who: Jeanne Bauwens and Jack J. Hourcade

What: LISTEN

Where: Bauwens, J. & Hourcade, J.J. (1989). Hey, would you just LISTEN. *Teaching Exceptional Children, 21*, 61.

When: Students need to focus on the teacher for directions or a lesson.

Why: A very common reason students are referred for special education services is that they "just don't listen." The ability to listen—to attend and respond appropriately—is a critical skill prerequisite to academic performance and success.

How: Use the following strategy to help students improve their listening skills:

L	=	**L**ook.
I	=	**I**dle your motor.
S	=	**S**it up straight.
T	=	**T**urn to me.
E	=	**E**ngage your brain.
N	=	**N**ow.

Teaching Tips

- List the six steps on cards and place them on students' desks, as well as on a wall chart for easy access and review.
- Initially, pause after saying each step to remind students of what they are learning to do.
- Once students have learned the steps, just say "Listen," and point to each of the LISTEN letters.
- Whenever possible, provide a reason for students to be listening (e.g., "Listen, please. The reason I want you to listen is that I am giving details about the field trip we will be taking next week").

Self-Monitoring Visual Prompt Strategy

Who: Mary Anne Prater, Rebecca Joy, Beth Chilman, Joan Temple, and Sidney R. Miller

What: Self-Monitoring Visual Prompt Strategy

Where: Prater, M.A., Joy, R., Chilman, B., Temple, J., & Miller, S.R. (1991). Self-monitoring of on-task behavior by adolescents with learning disabilities. *Learning Disability Quarterly, 14,* 164–177.

When: Students need to participate and listen in class.

Why: Many students are reluctant to participate in class because they have histories of repeated failure in school. Encouraging students to participate often has positive effects on attitudes toward school and subsequent achievement. This strategy will teach students to become more independent learners.

How: *Remember:*

1. Eyes on teacher or on work.

2. Sitting in seat;

   Facing forward;

   Feet on floor or legs crossed.

3. Using correct materials.

4. Working silently.

Teaching Tips

- Conduct instructional sessions at least three times a week.
- Describe each step in the strategy. Provide a reason for using it, give examples of situations in which it could be used, and describe the benefits of using it.
- Model each step of the strategy using verbal behaviors and overt actions, if appropriate.
- Have students practice the strategy.
- Provide supportive and corrective feedback, rewards, and praise.
- Teach the strategy with visual prompts.

Putting Theory Into Practice

Use a visual-prompt cue sheet:

	Eyes on teacher or on work.
	Sitting in seat; Facing forward; Feet on floor or legs crossed.
	Using correct materials.
	Working silently.

Have students use a self-monitoring sheet similar to this one to assist them in monitoring their on-/off-task behaviors.

Name: _____	
Date:_____	
Was I working?	
Yes ☐ ☐ ☐ ☐ ☐	
No ☐ ☐ ☐ ☐ ☐	

(adapted from Prater, Joy, Chilman, Temple, & Miller, p. 169)

SELF-POWER

Who: Nancy W. Sander, Deborah A. Bott, Charles Hughes, and Kathy Ruhl

What: SELF-POWER (a self-management strategy)

Where: Sander, N.W., Bott, D.A., Hughes, C., & Ruhl, K. (1991). Effects of a self-management strategy on task-independent behaviors of adolescents with learning disabilities. *B.C. Journal of Special Education, 15,* 64–75.

When: Students need to learn to monitor their own behaviors.

Why: Self-control is the ultimate goal of social skills interventions.

How:
P = **P**lan to change my behavior:

    S = **S**elect and define my goal.

    E = **E**stablish my goal and measure.

    L = **L**ist rewards and choose one.

    F = **F**ix the forms.

O = **O**bserve my behavior.

W = **W**rite it down.

E = **E**valuate my performance.

R = **R**eward myself.

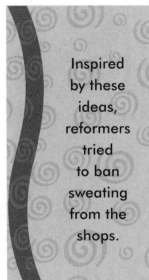

Inspired by these ideas, reformers tried to ban sweating from the shops.

Teaching Tips

- Conduct instructional sessions at least three times a week.
- Describe each step in the strategy. Provide a reason for using it, give examples of situations in which it could be used, and describe the benefits of using it.
- Model each step of the strategy using verbal behaviors and overt actions, if appropriate.
- Have students practice the strategy in controlled materials.
- Provide supportive and corrective feedback, rewards, and praise.

SECTION 3

What Now?

CHAPTER 8

SHARING WHAT YOU KNOW

The purpose of this chapter is to provide ideas for conducting learning strategies workshops for teachers. This chapter provides:

1. A strategy to use for planning workshops.

2. Content examples for a one-hour Mathematics Skills Learning Strategies Workshop, including suggestions for handouts (*also see* Blackline Masters for Overhead Transparencies, which correspond to the example workshop content).

3. Other information that may be helpful when conducting a workshop.

WORKSHOP Strategy

In keeping with the theme of this book, it was only appropriate to develop a strategy to explain the steps of conducting, and aid in planning, a learning strategies workshop:

W: <u>W</u>ork out a purpose.

O: <u>O</u>utline the workshop.

R: <u>R</u>ead up on the content.

K: <u>K</u>eep it simple.

S: <u>S</u>elect appropriate strategies to teach.

H: <u>H</u>andouts are a must.

O: <u>O</u>rganize materials.

P: <u>P</u>repare to have fun!

Here is an example of how to plan using the WORKSHOP Strategy:

W: *Work out a purpose.*

The purpose of this workshop is to provide participants with learning strategies to use in their classrooms. Strategies will address the areas of . . . (e.g., reading, written

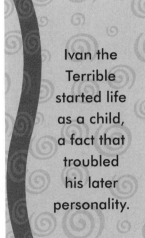

Ivan the Terrible started life as a child, a fact that troubled his later personality.

expression, mathematics, study skills). (Think about which content area you want to target for the audience. It may work better if you stick to just one content area rather than try to present too many at one time.) Methods will be described on how to implement the strategies in the classroom, and handouts will be provided.

- Participants will be able to define learning strategies.

- Participants will learn strategies to use in the areas of reading, written expression, mathematics, social skills, or study skills.

- Participants will be able to describe methods to teach specific learning strategies.

- Participants will be able to apply collaboration knowledge and skills when teaching and implementing strategies in inclusive classrooms.

- Participants will obtain a working list of strategies to use in the classroom.

O: <u>Outline</u> the workshop.

An outline is a great advance organizer for a workshop. The visual nature of an outline also provides a non-verbal representation of the overall structure of the presentation of information. Participants like to know what topics will be covered. A typical learning strategies workshop outline would illustrate the content to be covered and the organizational frame for covering it.

- Define learning strategies.
- Give an overview of methods to use to teach learning strategies.
- Use the STRATEGY Strategy (*see* Chapter 2, p. 16) and other suggestions in the sample workshop.
- Insert strategies from chapters that focus on reading, written expression, mathematics, study skills, or social skills.
- Discuss how to apply collaboration knowledge and skills when teaching and implementing strategies in inclusive classrooms.
- Provide a working list of strategies to use in the classroom.

R: Read up on the content.

Refer to the references for the strategies that will be presented, and include documentation on each reference so that participants can obtain additional information if desired. For a good source of general information on learning strategies, see:

Lambert, M. & Algozzine, B. (1998). The cognitive model. In L.J. O'Shea, D.J. O'Shea, and B. Algozzine, *Learning disabilities: From theory to practice* (pp. 257–281). Upper Saddle River, NJ: Prentice-Hall, Inc.

See also:

Cheek, E.H., Jr. & Cheek, M.C. (1983). *Reading instruction through content teaching.* Columbus, OH: Merrill.

Ellis, E.S., Deshler, D.D., Lenz, B.K., Schumaker, J.B., & Clark, F.L. (1991). An instructional model for teaching learning strategies. *Focus on Exceptional Children, 22*(6), 1–24.

Ellis, E.S. & Lenz, B.K. (1987). A component analysis of effective learning strategies for LD students. *Learning Disabilities Focus, 2*, 94–107.

Hoover, J.J. (1989). Study skills and the education of students with learning disabilities. *Journal of Learning Disabilities, 22*, 452–455, 461.

Lebzelter, S. & Nowacek, E.J. (1999). Reading strategies for secondary students with mild disabilities. *Intervention in School and Clinic, 34*, 212–219.

Mastropieri, M.A. & Scruggs, T.E. (1997). Best practices in promoting reading comprehension in students with learning disabilities: 1976–1996. *Remedial and Special Education, 18*, 197–222.

K: _Keep_ it simple.

Try to keep the content of the workshop simple. After giving an overview of characteristics of students with learning problems and how learning strategies relate to them, focus on specific strategies that teachers can use in their classrooms.

- The goal is to provide information that can be used "tomorrow."
- Use real-life examples, and identify ways to apply training.
- Summarize what has been learned.
- Request feedback on training.
- Identify where to obtain more information.

S: _Select_ appropriate strategies to teach.

Target specific strategies that the workshop participants will be able to use. Try not to overwhelm them by presenting too many strategies. Take time to teach the strategy, and walk through an example or two to ensure that teachers know how to use the strategy in their classrooms. Here are a few suggested strategies for specific skills development.

Reading Skills strategies:
- Critical Thinking Map (Idol, 1987)
- Five-Step Reading Comprehension Strategy (Schunk & Rice, 1987)
- POSSE (reading comprehension) (Englert & Mariage, 1990)
- Question-Answer Relationship (QAR) (Raphael, 1986)
- RARE: Reading for a Purpose (Gearheart, DeRuiter, & Sileo, 1986)

Written Expression Skills strategies:
- PLEASE (writing paragraphs) (Welch, 1992)
- Reportive Essay (writing essays) (Wong, Wong, Darlington, & Jones, 1991)
- STOP and DARE: Brainstorming (De La Paz & Graham, 1997)
- TREE (composing opinion essays) (Graham & Harris, 1989)

Mathematics Skills strategies:
- Arithmetic Problem Solving (Fleischner, Nuzum, & Marzola, 1987)
- Eight-Step Solving Strategy for Verbal Math Problems (Montague & Bos, 1986)
- Solving Simple Word Problems (Case, Harris, & Graham, 1992)
- Subtraction Using the "4Bs" Mnemonic Strategy (also use with addition) (Frank & Brown, 1992)

Study Skills strategies:
- IT FITS (mnemonic strategy) (King-Sears, Mercer, & Sindelar, 1992)
- PARS (study strategy) (Hoover, 1989)

H: <u>Handouts</u> are a must.

Provide handouts so that participants aren't bogged down with taking notes. It is especially important to provide handouts for strategies that are taught. Use a consistent format (e.g., who, what, why, and how) when preparing workshop handouts that focus on specific strategies (*see* Table 8.1).

- Keep each handout to a single page (two-sided, if necessary).
- Cover the strategy content in each handout, even if only in abbreviated form.
- Identify the source of each handout (i.e., workshop name, date, and place).

Berlin
was
airlifted
westward
and
divided
into
pieces.

O: *Organize materials.*

This is the key to an effective workshop. Brainstorm a list of materials that are needed, such as an overhead projector, overhead pens, transparencies, a computer and a projector for PowerPoint® presentations, flipcharts with plenty of paper, markers, enough handouts for participants, and extra paper for activities. *If you think you might need it, take it and, have a backup plan in case something goes wrong.*

- Planning ahead is a measure of class.
- Plan breaks and stick to the plan.
- Plan for discussion and stick to the plan.

P: *Prepare to have fun!*

Enjoy what you are doing and have fun with the workshop. Start out with an icebreaker activity, and plan some fun activities among the technical strategy presentations. Give participants opportunities to try out the strategies.

- Fun is a good thing—ask anybody!
- Are we having fun yet?
- If you're happy and you know it, clap your hands.

To help you get started, the remaining pages of this chapter provide examples of content that could be included in a Mathematics Skills Learning Strategies Workshop. If you would like to use corresponding overheads for this workshop, refer to the Blackline Masters for Overhead Transparencies section of the book.

CONTENT EXAMPLE

The following are sample slides that can be used with a PowerPoint workshop presentation

> ## *Topic: Improving Mathematics Skills With Learning Strategies*
>
> **Characteristics of Students With Math Difficulties**
> - Early indications of math problems—concepts of quantity.
> - Disturbances of spatial relationships.
> - Disturbances of motor and visual perceptions.
> - Language and reading problems.
> - Poor concepts of direction and time.
> - Memory problems.

> **Math Skills of Students With Learning Disabilities**
> - Incomplete mastery of basic facts.
> - Reversing numbers.
> - Confusing operational symbols.
> - Copying problems incorrectly from one line to another.
> - Difficulty recalling the sequence of operational processes.
> - Inability to understand and retain abstract concepts.
> - Difficulty comprehending word problems.
> - Reasoning deficits.

> **What Is a Learning Strategy?**
> - A learning strategy is how we think and act.
> - Learning strategy instruction teaches students to use certain steps when performing specific tasks (e.g., solving mathematical word problems).

Purpose: To provide participants with learning strategies to use in improving mathematics skills of students with learning disabilities.

CONTENT EXAMPLE

Addition Using the SASH Mnemonic Strategy

Teaching Students How to Add

S = **S**tart in the 1s column.

A = **A**dd the numerals together.

S = **Sh**ould I carry a numeral?

H = **H**ave I carried the correct numeral?

Frank, A.R. & Brown, D. (1992). Self-monitoringstrategies in arithmetic. *Teaching Exceptional Children, 24* (2), 52 - 53.

Subtraction Using the "4Bs" Mnemonic Strategy
Teaching Students How to Subtract

- **B**egin?   In the 1s column.

- **B**igger?   Which number is bigger?

- **B**orrow?   If bottom number is bigger,
                       I must borrow.

- **B**asic Facts?   Remember them. (Use Touch Math,
                       if needed.)

Frank, A.R. & Brown, D. (1992). Self-monitoringstrategies in arithmetic. *Teaching Exceptional Children, 24* (2), 52 - 53.

CONTENT EXAMPLE

Multiplication Facts Strategy

Teaching Students Basic Multiplication Facts

1. Point to the number you can count by.

2. Make hash marks for the other numbers.

3. Count by the number, and point once for each hash mark.

4. Write down the last number you said.

Lloyd, J.W., Saltzman, N.J., & Kauffman, J.M. (1981). Predictable generalization in academic learning as a result of pre-skills and strategy training. *Learning Disability Quarterly, 4,* 203 - 216.

Division Facts Strategy

Teaching Students Basic Division Facts

1. Point to the divisor.

2. Count by the divisor until you get the number of the dividend.

3. Make hash marks while counting by.

4. Count the number of hash marks.

5. Write down the number of hash marks.

Lloyd, J.W., Saltzman, N.J., & Kauffman, J.M. (1981). Predictable generalization in academic learning as a result of pre-skills and strategy training. *Learning Disability Quarterly, 4,* 203 - 216.

CONTENT EXAMPLE

Math Problem Solving I Strategy

Teaching Students to Solve Mathematical Word Problems

1. **Read** (for understanding).

2. **Paraphrase** (your own words).

3. **Visualize** (a picture or a diagram).

4. **Hypothesize** (a plan to solve the problem).

5. **Estimate** (predict the answer).

6. **Compute** (do the arithmetic).

7. **Check** (make sure everything is right).

Montague, M. (1992). The effects of cognitive and metacognitive strategy instruction on the mathematical problem solving of middle school students with learning disabilities. *Journal of Learning Disabilities, 25*, 230 - 248.

Arithmetic Problem Solving Strategy

Teaching Students to Solve Mathematical Word Problems

1. **READ:**	What is the question?
2. **REREAD:**	What is the necessary information?
3. **THINK:**	Putting together? (*Add*)
	Taking apart? (*Subtract*)
	Do I need all the information?
	Is it a two-step problem?
4. **SOLVE:**	Write the equation.
5. **CHECK:**	Recalculate.
	Label.
	Compare.

Fleischner, J.E., Nuzum, M.B., & Marzola, E.S. (1987). Devising an instructional program to teach arithmetic problem-solving skills to students with learning disabilities. *Journal of Learning Disabilities, 20*, 214 - 217.

CONTENT EXAMPLE

Solving Word Problems Strategy

Teaching Students to Solve Mathematical Word Problems

1. Read the problem.

2. <u>Underline</u> or **highlight** key words, sentences, or questions.

3. Decide what sign to use.

4. Set up the problem.

5. Solve the problem.

Karrison, J. & Carroll, M. (1991). Solving word problems. *Teaching Exceptional Children, 23* (4), 55 - 56.

Solving Simple Word Problems Strategy

Teaching Students to Solve Mathematical Word Problems

1. Read the problem out loud.

2. Look for important words, and circle them.

3. Draw pictures to help tell what is happening.

4. Write down the math sentence.

5. Write down the answer.

Case, L.P., Harris, K.R., & Graham, S. (1992). Improving the mathematical problem-solving skills of students with learning disabilities: Self-regulated strategy development. *The Journal of Special Education, 26*, 1 - 19.

CONTENT EXAMPLE

*Completing Math Problems Using
the SOLVE Strategy*

**When Students Need a Mnemonic Strategy to Solve Addition,
Subtraction, Multiplication, and Division Problems**

S = <u>S</u>ee the sign.

O = <u>O</u>bserve and answer (if unable to answer,
keep going).

L = <u>L</u>ook and draw.

V = <u>V</u>erify your answer.

E = <u>E</u>nter your answer.

Miller, S.P. & Mercer, C.D. (1993). Mnemonics: Enhancing math performance
of students with learning difficulties. *Intervention in School and Clinic, 29*, 78 - 82.

STRATEGY Strategy

Suggested Teaching Sequence

S = <u>S</u>tart with an appraisal of the current problem,
and identify a strategy to solve it.

T = <u>T</u>each the strategy using specific, direct instruction.

R = <u>R</u>ehearse and model each component of the strategy.

A = <u>A</u>rrange practice sessions with controlled materials.

T = <u>T</u>ry the strategy with actual classroom materials.

E = <u>E</u>ngage in frequent feedback.

G = <u>G</u>ive frequent opportunities to use the strategy.

Y = <u>Y</u>ield evaluation data after using the strategy.

CONTENT EXAMPLE

Teaching Tips

- Teach students to use word-problem strategies to solve one-, two-, and three-step word problems.

- Problems can be solved orally or on paper.

- Limit the number of problems assigned, and have students show their work to ensure that they are completing each step of the strategy.

- Highlight key words in word problems.

- Use graph paper to line up math problems.

More Teaching Tips

- Use highlighters to visually note mathematical signs.
- Teach students how to check their answers.
- Put sample problems and their answer sequences on a sheet for students to put in their notebooks as a reference.
- Write the strategy steps on a cue card (index card or bookmark) and use to help solve problems.
- Put the strategy steps on a bulletin board.
- Do not overwhelm students with too many strategies at once.

CONTENT EXAMPLE

What Have We Learned?

- Many students experience problems learning mathematics.
- Learning strategies are ways to complete tasks.
- Learning strategies exist for improving math skills.
- Effective steps for teaching learning strategies are well documented.
- Learning strategies work!

For More Information:

University of Kansas
Center for Research on Learning
Strategic Instruction Model
www.ku-crl.org/htmlfiles/sim.html

NICHCY
P.O. Box 1492
Washington, D.C. 20013
1-800-695-0285
www.nichcy.org

Dr. Monica Lambert
Appalachian State University
lambertma@appstate.edu

HANDOUT EXAMPLE

Table 8.1 Sample Handout for Mathematics Learning Strategies Workshop

Mathematics

SASH Mnemonic Strategy	(Frank & Brown, 1992)	S = <u>S</u>tart in the 1s column. A = <u>A</u>dd the numerals together. S = <u>S</u>hould I carry a numeral? H = <u>H</u>ave I carried the correct numeral?

Subtraction Using the "4Bs" Mnemonic Strategy	(Frank & Brown, 1992)	**Begin**? In the 1s column.
		Bigger? Which number is bigger?
		Borrow? If bottom number is bigger,
		     I must borrow.
		Basic Facts? Remember them.
		     (Use Touch Math, if needed.)

Multiplication Facts Strategy	(Lloyd, Saltzman, & Kauffman, 1981)	1. Point to the number you can count by. 2. Make hash marks for the other numbers. 3. Count by the number, and point once for each hash mark. 4. Write down the last number you said.
Division Facts Strategy	(Lloyd, Saltzman, & Kauffman, 1981)	1. Point to the divisor. 2. Count by the divisor until you get the number of the dividend. 3 Make hash marks while counting by. 4. Count the number of hash marks. 5. Write down the number of hash marks.
Math Problem Montague, 1992) **Solving I Strategy**		1. **Read** (for understanding). 2. **Paraphrase** (your own words). 3. **Visualize** (a picture or a diagram). 4. **Hypothesize** (a plan to solve the problem). 5. **Estimate** (predict the answer). 6. **Compute** (do the arithmetic). 7. **Check** (make sure everything is right).

Arithmetic Problem Solving Strategy	(Fleischner, Nuzum & Marzola, 1987)	1. **READ**: What is the question? 2. **REREAD**: What is the necessary information? 3. **THINK**: Putting together? (*Add*) Taking apart? (*Subtract*) Do I need all the information? Is it a two-step problem? 4. **SOLVE**: Write the equation. 5. **CHECK**: Recalculate. Label Compare.
Solving Word Problems Strategy	(Karrison & Carroll, 1991)	1. Read the problem. 2. <u>Underline</u> or **highlight** key words, sentences, or questions. 3. Decide what sign to use. 4. Set up the problem. 5. Solve the problem.
Solving Simple Word Problems Strategy	(Case, Harris, & Graham, 1992)	1. Read the problem out loud. 2. Look for important words, and circle them. 3. Draw pictures to help tell what is happening. 4. Write down the math sentence. 5. Write down the answer.
SOLVE Strategy	(Miller & Mercer, 1993)	S = <u>S</u>ee the sign. O = <u>O</u>bserve and answer. L = <u>L</u>ook and draw. V = <u>V</u>erify your answer. E = <u>E</u>nter your answer.

HANDOUT EXAMPLE

For More Information:

Case, L.P., Harris, K.R., & Graham, S. (1992). Improving the mathematical problem-solving skills of students with learning disabilities: Self-regulated strategy development. *The Journal of Special Education, 26*, 1–19.

Fleischner, J.E., Nuzum, M. B., & Marzola, E.S. (1987). Devising an instructional program to teach arithmetic problem-solving skills to students with learning disabilities. *Journal of Learning Disabilities, 20*, 214–217.

Frank, A.R., & Brown, D. (1992). Self-monitoring strategies in arithmetic. *Teaching Exceptional Children, 24*(2), 52–53.

Karrison, J., & Carroll, M. (1991). Solving word problems. *Teaching Exceptional Children, 23*(4), 55–56.

Lloyd, J.W., Saltzman, N.J., & Kauffman, J.M. (1981). Predictable generalization in academic learning as a result of pre-skills and strategy training. *Learning Disability Quarterly, 4*, 203–216.

Miller, S.P., & Mercer, C.D. (1991). *Addition facts 0 to 9*. Lawrence, KS: Edge Enterprises.

Miller, S.P., & Mercer, C.D. (1993). Mnemonics: Enhancing math performance of students with learning difficulties. *Intervention in School and Clinic, 29*, 78–82.

Montague, M. (1992). The effects of cognitive and metacognitive strategy instruction on the mathematical problem solving of middle school students with learning disabilities. *Journal of Learning Disabilities, 25*, 230–248.

CHAPTER 9

CLOSING THOUGHTS: RESOURCES AND GENERAL TEACHING SUGGESTIONS

The mission is almost accomplished. The end is near. What more can we say? Before closing the book on learning strategies, we thought we should provide some information on other resources that are available on learning strategies and reiterate the effective teaching practices for providing instruction in learning strategies. It seems a good way to finish.

What Resources Are Available?

We wrote this book as a resource for people who are interested in using learning strategies to improve academic and social performance of all students. Not all learning strategies ever developed or demonstrated to be effective are included in this collection, and we do not intend the book to be a substitute for professional training in the use of learning strategies. Our intention is to provide a simple, systematic, structured presentation of useful information for individuals who are interested in talking with colleagues, students, and parents about learning strategies. Other resources are available if you are interested in more information about learning strategies or learning strategies training.

Spelling Strategies

We did not review strategies for improving spelling skills. Mushinski Fulk and Stormont-Spurgin (1995) provide a review of interventions that resulted in improved spelling performance for students with learning disabilities. They present 14 practical teacher-directed and student study strategies for optimizing spelling instruction. These techniques are easy to implement and require minimal preparation time. Here are a couple of examples of systematic study procedures that include three-step and five-step strategies:

The Holy Omen Empire soon collapsed like a pack of cards.

Three-Step Study Strategy (Pratt-Struthers, Struthers, & Williams, 1983)

    1. Copy the word.

    2. Write the word from memory.

    3. Compare the word with the model.

Five-Step Study Strategy (Graham & Freeman, 1985)

    1. Say the word.

    2. Write and say the word.

    3. Check the word.

    4. Trace and say the word.

    5. Write the word from memory and check spelling.

Five-Step Study Strategy (Graham & Freeman, 1985)

    1. Trace the word.

    2. Write the word.

    3. Check the word.

    4. Reinforce yourself, or

    5. Correct your spelling.

National Information Center for Children and Youth With Disabilities

The National Information Center for Children and Youth with Disabilities (NICHCY) is an information and referral center serving the United States, Puerto Rico, and the U.S. Territories. NICHCY provides families, students, educators, and others with information on disability-related topics regarding children and youth, from birth through age 21. Anyone may contact NICHCY for information (www.nichcy.org). Many of their materials are available in Spanish and are also available in alternative formats, such as on disk. NICHCY has two general resources related to learning strategies:

1. *Interventions for Students with Learning Disabilities* (News Digest #25) focuses on helping students to develop their use of learning strategies.

2. *Learning Strategies for Students with Learning Disabilities* (Bibliography 14) lists selected journal articles and books available on learning strategies for these students.

This information is copyright-free, unless otherwise indicated, and professionals are encouraged to copy and share it (with credit to the National Information Center for Children and Youth with Disabilities). NICHCY is a great resource for materials to distribute as part of a learning strategies workshop. For example, the following resources are listed as "Strategies for Mathematics" and would form an excellent basis for a handout for a Mathematics Learning Strategies Workshop:

Bley, N.S., & Thornton, C.A. (1994). *Teaching mathematics to students with learning disabilities* (3rd ed.). Austin, TX: Pro-Ed.

Brigham, F.J., Wilson, R., Jones, E., & Moisio, M. (1996, Spring). Best practices: Teaching decimals, fractions, and percents to students with learning disabilities. *LD Forum, 21*(3), 10–15.

Case, L.P. (1992, Spring). Improving the mathematical problem-solving skills of students with learning disabilities: Self-regulated strategy development. *Journal of Special Education, 26*, 1–19.

Chinn, S.J., & Ashcroft, J.R. (1993). *Mathematics for dyslexics*: A teaching handbook. San Diego: Singular.

Cooper, R. (1994). Alternative math techniques instructional guide. Bryn Mawr, PA: Center for Alternative Learning. (ERIC Document Reproduction Service No. ED 376 355.)

Corral, N., & Antia, S.D. (1997, March/April). Self talk: Strategies for success in math. *TEACHING Exceptional Children, 29*(4), 42–45.

Dunn, C., & Rabren, K. (1996, Spring). Functional mathematics instruction to prepare students for adulthood. *LD Forum, 21*(3), 34–40.

Jitendra, A., & Xin, Y.P. (1997, Winter). Mathematical word-problem-solving instruction for students with mild disabilities and students at risk for math failure: A research synthesis. *Journal of Special Education, 30*, 412–438.

Kelly, B., & Carnine, D. (1996, Spring). Teaching problem-solving strategies for word problems to students with learning disabilities. *LD Forum, 21*(3), 5–9.

Lambert, M.A. (1996, Winter). Mathematics textbooks, materials, and manipulatives. *LD Forum, 21*(2), 41–45.

Lock, R.H. (1996, Winter). Adapting mathematics instruction in the general education classroom for students with mathematics disabilities. *LD Forum, 21*(2), 19–23.

Miles, D.D., & Forcht, J.P. (1995, November). Mathematics strategies for secondary students with learning disabilities or mathematics deficiencies: A cognitive approach. *Intervention in School and Clinic, 31*(2), 91–96.

Miller, A.D., Barbetta, P.M., Drevno, G.E., Martz, S.A., & Heron, T.E. (1996, Spring). Math peer tutoring for students with specific learning disabilities. *LD Forum, 21*(3), 21–28.

Miller, S.P., & Mercer, C.D. (1993, November). Mnemonics: Enhancing the math performance of students with learning disabilities. *Intervention in School and Clinic, 29*(2), 78–82.

Miller, S.P., Strawser, S., & Mercer, C.D. (1996, Winter). Promoting strategic math performance among students with learning disabilities. *LD Forum, 21*(2), 34–40.

Montague, M. (1993). Cognitive strategy instruction and mathematical problem-solving performance of students with learning disabilities. *Learning Disabilities Research and Practice, 8*, 223–232.

Montague, M. (1995, Spring). Cognitive instruction and mathematics: Implications for students with learning disabilities. *Focus on Learning Problems in Mathematics, 17*(2), 39–49.

Rivera, D.P. (1996, Spring). Using cooperative learning to teach mathematics to students with learning disabilities. *LD Forum, 21*(3), 29–33.

Rivera, D.P. (Ed.). (1996a, Winter). Teaching math to students with learning disabilities: Part I (Special issue). *LD Forum, 21*(2).

Rivera, D.P. (Ed.). (1996b, Spring). Teaching math to students with learning disabilities: Part II (Special issue). *LD Forum, 21*(3).

Salend, S.J., & Hofstetter, E. (1996, March). Adapting a problem-solving approach to teaching mathematics to students with mild disabilities. *Intervention in School and Clinic, 31*, 209–217.

Scott, P.B., & Raborn, D.T. (1996, Winter). Realizing the gifts of diversity among students with learning disabilities. *LD Forum, 21*(2), 10–18.

Strategic Instruction Model (SIM)—University of Kansas

Over a period of more than 20 years, researchers at the University of Kansas have developed the Strategic Instruction Model (SIM). This comprehensive instructional system encompasses revised curriculum materials that take into account different learning styles, routines that teachers can use to address the needs of learners in their classrooms, and specific steps that at-risk individuals can follow to improve their chances of academic success. The University of Kansas Center for Research on Learning provides professional training experiences throughout the year for those interested in learning more about the Strategic Instruction Model and its components.

The university's Learning Strategies Curriculum includes strategies related to storing and remembering information, expressing information, reading, mathematics, demonstrating competence, and social interaction. Components within each area are described in the following sections.

Strategies related to storing and remembering information. The FIRST-Letter Mnemonic Strategy and the Paired Associates Strategy focus on helping students remember information. The LINCS Vocabulary Strategy focuses on helping students learn the meaning of new words.

Strategies related to expressing information. The Error Monitoring Strategy helps students identify and correct mistakes in written products. The InSPECT Strategy helps students identify and correct mistakes in written products using technology aids. The Sentence Writing Strategy (including the Fundamentals in the Sentence Writing Strategy and the Proficiency in the Sentence Writing Strategy) helps students craft well-constructed sentences. The Paragraph Writing Strategy helps students write well-constructed paragraphs.

Strategies related to reading. The Paraphrasing Strategy focuses on reading a limited selection of material, identifying the main idea and the details of the selection, and putting the information into the student's own words. The Self-Questioning Strategy focuses on asking questions about information in a selection of reading material and then reading the selection to answer the questions. The Visual Imagery Strategy focuses on reading short selections and visualizing what is described. The Word Identification Strategy focuses on decoding unknown words in reading materials.

Strategies related to mathematics. The Addition and Subtraction Strategies help students improve place-value skills and solve basic addition and subtraction problems using numbers from 0 to 18. The Multiplication and Division Strategies help students solve multiplication and division problems using numbers from 0 to 81.

Strategies related to demonstrating competence. The Assignment Completion Strategy focuses on keeping track of school assignments. The Test-Taking Strategy focuses on allocating time, reading instructions and questions carefully, and identifying unanswered questions during tests.

Strategies related to social interaction. Community Building Series: Talking Together helps students participate appropriately in class discussions; Following Instructions Together helps students follow directions. Cooperative Thinking Strategies: The BUILD Strategy helps students analyze and resolve issues in groups; The LEARN Strategy helps students learn information in groups; SCORE: Social Skills for Cooperative Groups helps students act appropriately in groups; The Teamwork Strategy helps students organize and complete projects in groups; and The THINK Strategy helps students solve problems in groups. The Self-Advocacy Strategy helps students participate effectively in conferences. SLANT: A Starter Strategy for Class Participation helps students participate in class discussions.

For more information on the University of Kansas Learning Strategies Curriculum, teacher training, and how to implement strategies instruction throughout a school, contact:

The University of Kansas

Center for Research on Learning

Joseph R. Pearson Hall

1122 W. Campus Rd., Rm. 521

Lawrence, KS 66045-3101

(785) 864-4780

crl@ku.edu or www.ku-crl.org

An excellent brochure is available that describes key features of the Strategic Instruction Model (www.ku-crl.org/htmlfiles/simbrochure.pdf); this brochure would be an excellent workshop handout.

Revisiting Strategy Instruction

Much has been written about using learning strategies to improve skills of students with disabilities. Harris and Pressley (1991) indicate three critical points in strategy instruction:

First, strategy instruction is and continues to grow as an important area in the field of research. This means that more research will be conducted in strategies instruction and in how to apply it to content areas. It also means that strategy instruction will be incorporated into general education classrooms. This will provide an environment for strategy generalization and also assist students without disabilities.

Second, strategy instruction is not a panacea. There are limitations to using strategies. Strategy instruction allows teachers to address the needs of students by providing a step-by-step process for approaching tasks. Strategies should be used when they meet the individual needs of the student, if they assist in remediating the student's problem, if they appear to be the best solution, and if teachers are able to teach the strategy effectively.

Third, good strategy instruction is not just memorizing the steps. Good strategy instruction incorporates teaching students why they are learning a strategy, how it will help them, when to use the strategy, and which settings are appropriate for the use of the strategy. Students need to be actively involved in all stages of the strategy instruction. The teacher's role is to describe the strategy, model the strategy, provide practice and modify the strategy, and reteach when necessary.

Effective teachers use the following steps when implementing interventions based on the learning strategies model:

Step 1: Assess student strategy usage for a specified task.

Step 2: Teach students a strategy related to the task.

Step 3: Practice using the strategy and evaluate proficiency.

Step 4: Apply the strategy in various settings.

Step 5: Evaluate use and modify for application in other settings.

Step 6: Teach students to design their own strategies:

    a. Select a task that needs a strategy.

    b. Break the task into component parts.

    c. Devise a mnemonic or other method to remember the strategy steps.

    d. Apply the strategy to the task.

    e. Modify the steps, if necessary (include self-monitoring and self-questioning when appropriate).

WHWAOG (We Hope We Accomplished Our Goal)

We wrote this book for professionals who are interested in finding effective ways to keep students actively involved in their own learning. We also wrote this book for anyone interested in learning about learning strategies. We see it as a first step in bringing selected evidence-based practices to practitioners, and this means that the end is just the beginning.

Literature ran wild. Writers expressed themselves with cymbals.

POSTSCRIPT

The Intention of All This

On October 2, 2001, President George W. Bush ordered the creation of the 24-member President's Commission on Excellence in Special Education (Executive Order 13227). The President charged the Commission with studying issues related to federal, state, and local special education programs in order to improve the educational performance of students with disabilities.

The Commission held 13 open hearings and meetings across the country. At those meetings and hearings, the members heard from 109 expert witnesses and more than 175 parents, teachers, students with disabilities, and members of the public. Hundreds of other individuals provided the Commission with letters, written statements, and research.

The Commission's effort represents the most expansive review of special education in the 27-year history of federal special education legislation. The Commission submitted a report titled, "A New Era: Revitalizing Special Education for Children and Their Families," to the White House on July 1, 2002, as required by the Executive Order. One finding of all the analyses and testimony was that the system of special education "does not always embrace or implement evidence-based practices" (Executive Summary, Finding 8, p. 7). The message here is that professionals in special education have a knowledge base of what to do to improve the lives of individuals with disabilities, but these methods are not always used. The importance of the indictment is evident in its relation to the second of three recommendations by the Commission: "Reforms must move the system toward . . . swift intervention, using scientifically based instruction and teaching methods." (Executive Summary, Major Recommendation 2, p. 8.)

Interestingly, the Commission's report did not provide a list of the evidence-based practices that were being used—or not being used—so the indictment and its directed recommendation bear little chance of being followed by action or improving special education practices. The intention, however, is a good one: When

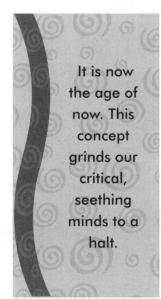

It is now the age of now. This concept grinds our critical, seething minds to a halt.

children are failing to profit from the educational menu of experiences provided in their schools, move swiftly to them with instruction and teaching methods that work.

Learning strategy instruction works. The ultimate goal of learning strategies instruction is to teach students a skill that is needed at the present time and to generalize the skill across situations and settings at various times. Learning strategies teach students a step-by-step process for completing a learning task that allows the student to become an active part in the learning process. Learning strategies instruction uses an effective teaching model that proceeds from pretest/description to posttest/generalization stages using demonstration, rehearsal, practice, and feedback as its primary teaching methods.

Initially, strategies are learned in a specific context and are used only in that context. After the student is more proficient in strategy usage, he or she can think about the strategies and learn to use them for other tasks. There is a research base to support the use of learning strategies to improve reading, writing, computing, studying, and performing appropriately in social situations. The challenge—making it happen—remains.

We hope the information we have provided in our book will inspire you to use learning strategies, demonstrate that learning strategies are effective, and/or learn more about learning strategies . . . "**We Gave It Our Best Shot**" (WeGIOBS).

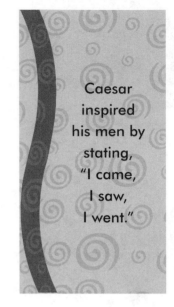

Caesar inspired his men by stating, "I came, I saw, I went."

BLACKLINE MASTERS

For Overhead Transparencies

What Are Learning Strategies?

◎ A learning strategy is how we think and act. Learning strategy instruction teaches students steps to use when performing specific tasks (e.g., solving mathematical word problems).

Improving Mathematics Skills with Learning Strategies

◎

◎Purpose:

To provide participants with learning strategies to use in improving mathematics skills of students with learning disabilities.

Characteristics of Students With Math Difficulties

- Early Indications of math problems—concepts of quality.

- Disturbances of spatial relationships.

- Disturbances of motor and visual perceptions

- Language and reading problems.

- Poor concepts of direction and time.

- Memory problems.

Mercer, C.D. (1997). *Students with learning disabilities* (5th ed.) Upper Saddle River, NJ: Merrill.

Math Skills of Students With Learning Disabilities

- Incomplete mastery of basic facts.

- Reversing numbers.

- Confusing operational symbols.

- Copying problems incorrectly from one line to another.

- Difficulty recalling the sequence of operational processes.

- Inability to understand and retain abstract concepts.

- Difficulty comprehending word problems

- Reasoning deficits.

Mercer, C.D. (1997). *Students with learning disabilities* (5th ed.) Upper Saddle River, NJ: Merrill.

Addition Using the SASH Mnemonic Strategy

Teaching Students How to Add

🌀 **S** = **Start** in the 1s column.

🌀 **A** = **Add** the numerals together.

🌀 **S** = **Should** I carry a numeral?

🌀 **H** = **Have** I carried the correct numeral?

Frank, A.R. & Brown, D. (1992). Self-monitoring strategies in arithmetic. *Teaching Exceptional Children, 24*(2), 52–53.

Subtraction Using the "4Bs" Mnemonic Strategy

Teaching Students How to Add

⊚ **Begin**? In the 1s column.

⊚ **Bigger**? Which number is bigger?

⊚ **Borrow**? If bottom number is bigger, I must borrow.

⊚ **Basic** Facts? Remember them. (Use Touch Math, if needed.)

Frank, A.R. & Brown, D. (1992). Self-monitoring strategies in arithmetic. *Teaching Exceptional Children, 24*(2), 52–53.

Multiplication Facts Strategy

Teaching Students Basic Multiplication Facts

1. Point to the number you can count by.

2. Make hash marks for the other numbers.

3. Count by the number, and point once for each hash mark.

4. Write down the last number said.

Lloyd, J.W., Saltzman, N.J., & Kauffman, J.M. (1981). Predictable generalization in academic learning as a result of pre-skills and strategy training. *Learning Disability Quarterly, 4*, 203–216.

Division Facts Strategy

Teaching Students Basic Division Facts

1. Point to the divisor.

2. Count by the divisor until you get the number of the dividend.

3. Make hash marks while counting by.

4. Count the number of hash marks.

5. Write down the number of hash marks.

Lloyd, J.W., Saltzman, N.J., & Kauffman, J.M. (1981). Predictable generalization in academic learning as a result of pre-skills and strategy training. *Learning Disability Quarterly, 4*, 203–216.

Math Problem Solving I Strategy

Teaching Students to Solve Mathematical Word Problems

1. **Read** (for understanding).

2. **Paraphrase** (your own words).

3. **Visualize** (a picture or a diagram).

4. **Hypothesize** (a plan to solve the problem).

5. **Estimate** (predict the answer).

6. **Compute** (do the arithmetic).

7. **Check** (make sure everything is right).

Montague, M. (1992). The effects of cognitive and metacognitive strategy instruction on the mathematical problem solving of middle school students with learning disabilities. *Journal of Learning Disabilities, 25,* 230–248.

Arithmetic Problem Solving Strategy

Teaching Students to Solve Mathematical Word Problems

1. **READ:** What is the question?

2. **REREAD:** What is the necessary information?

3. **THINK:** Putting together? (*Add*)
   Taking apart? (*Subtract*)
   Do I need all the information?
   Is it a two-step problem?

4. **SOLVE:** Write the equation.

5. **CHECK:** Recalculate, Label, Compare.

Fleischner, J.E., Nuzum, M.B., & Marzola, E.S. (1987). Devising an instructional program to teach arithmetic problem-solving skills to students with learning disabilities, *Journal of Learning Disabilities, 20*, 214–217.

Solving Word Problems Strategy

Teaching Students to Solve

Mathematical Word Problems

1. Read the problem.

2. <u>Underline</u> or **highlight** key words, sentences, or questions.

3. Decide what sign to use.

4. Set up the problem.

5. Solve the problem.

Karrison, J. Carroll, M. (1991). Solving word problems. *Teaching Exceptional Children, 23*(4), 55–56.

Solving Simple Word Problems Strategy

Teaching Students to Solve Mathematical Word Problems

1. Read the problem out loud.

2. Look for important words, and circle them.

3. Draw pictures to help tell what is happening.

4. Write down the math sentence.

5. Write down the answer.

Case, L. P., Harris, K.R., & Graham, S. S. (1991). Improving the mathematical problem-solving skills of students with learning disabilities: Self-regulated strategy development. *The Journal of Special Education, 26,* 1–19.

Completing Math Problems Using the SOLVE Strategy

When Students Need a Mnemonic Strategy to Solve Addition, Subtraction, Multiplication, and Division Problems

S = **See** the sign.

O = **Observe** and answer (if unable to answer, keep going).

L = **Look** and draw.

V = **Verify** your answer.

E = **Enter** your answer.

Miller, S. P. & Mercer, C.D. (1993). Mnemonics: Enhancing math performance of students with learning difficulties. *Intervention in Shcool and Clinic. 29,* 78–82.

STRATEGY Strategy

Suggested Teaching Sequence

S = **S**tart with an appraisal of the current problem, and identify a strategy to solve it.

T = **T**each the strategy using specific, direct instruction.

R = **R**ehearse and model each component of the strategy.

A = **A**rrange practice sessions with controlled materials.

T = **T**ry the strategy with actual classroom materials.

E = **E**ngage in frequent feedback.

G = **G**ive frequent opportunities to use the strategy.

Y = **Y**ield evaluation data after using the strategy.

Teaching Tips

- Teach students to use the word-problem strategies to solve one-, two-, and three-step word problems.

- Problems can be solved orally or on paper.

- Limit the number of problems assigned, and have students show their work to ensure that they are completing each step on the strategy.

- Highlight key words in word problems.

- Use graph paper to line up math problems.

More Teaching Tips

- Use highlighters to visually note mathematical signs.

- Teach students how to check their answers.

- Put sample problems and their answer sequences on a sheet for students to put in their notebooks as a reference.

- Write the strategy steps on a cue card (index card or bookmark) and use to help solve problems.

- Put the strategy steps on a bulletin board.

- Do not overwhelm students with too many strategies at once.

What Have We Learned?

- Many students experience problems learning mathematics.

- Learning strategies are ways to complete tasks.

- Learning strategies exist for improving math skills.

- Effective steps for teaching learning strategies are well documented.

- Learning strategies work!

For More Information

@ University of Kansas

Center for Research on Learning

Strategic Instruction Model

www.ku-crl.org/htmlfiles/sim.html

@ NICHCY

P.O. Box 1492

Washington, D.C. 20013

1-800-695-0285

www.nichcy.org

@ Dr. Monica Lambert

Appalachian State University

lambertma@appstate.edu

REFERENCES

References

Boudah, D.J., & O'Neill, K.J. (1999). *Learning strategies.* Arlington, Va.: ERIC Clearinghouse on Disabilities and Gifted Education, The Council for Exceptional Children. ERIC/OSEP Digest E577. Retrieved Jan. 1, 2002, from http://www.ericec.org/digests/e577.html.

Bulgren, J.A., Hock, M.F., Schumaker, J.B., & Deshler, D.D. (1995). The effects of instruction in a paired associates strategy on the information mastery performance of students with learning disabilities. *Learning Disabilities Research and Practice, 10*(1), 22–37.

Clark, F.L., Deshler, D.D., Schumaker, J.B., Alley, G.R., & Warner, M.M. (1984). Visual imagery and self-questioning: Strategies to improve comprehension of written material. *Journal of Learning Disabilities, 17*(3), 145–149.

Davidson, G.V., & Smith, P.L. (1990). Instructional design considerations for learning strategies instruction. *International Journal of Instructional Media, 17,* 227–244.

De La Paz, S., & Graham, S. (1997). Strategy instruction in planning: Effects on the writing performance and behavior of students with learning difficulties. *Exceptional Children, 63,* 167–181.

Ellis, E.S., (1994). Integrating writing strategy instruction with content-area instruction: Part 1—Orienting students to organizational devices. *Intervention in School and Clinic, 29*(3), 169–179.

Ellis, E.S., Deshler, D.D., Lenz, B.K., Schumaker, J.B., & Clark, F.L. (1991). An instructional model for teaching learning strategies. *Focus on Exceptional Children, 22*(6), 1–24.

Ellis, E.S. & Lenz, B.K. (1987). A component analysis of effective learning strategies for LD students. *Learning Disabilities Focus, 2,* 94–107.

Ellis, E.S., Lenz, B.K., & Sabornie, E.J. (1987a). Generalization and adaptation of learning strategies to natural environments: Part 1: Critical agents. *Remedial and Special Education, 8*(1), 6–20.

Ellis, E.S., Lenz, B.K., & Sabornie, E.J. (1987b). Generalization and adaptation of learning strategies to natural environments: Part 2: Research into practice. *Remedial and Special Education, 8*(2), 6–23.

Forness, S.R., Kavale, K.A., Blum, I.M., & Lloyd, J.W. (1997). Mega-analysis of meta-analysis: What works in special education and related services. *Teaching Exceptional Children, 29*(6), 4–9.

Fulk, B.M., & Stormont-Spurgin, M. (1995). Fourteen spelling strategies for students with learning disabilities. *Intervention in School and Clinic, 31*(1), 1–16.

Gearheart, B.R., DeRuiter, J.A., & Sileo, T.W. (1986). *Teaching mildly and moderately handicapped students.* Englewood Cliffs, NJ: Prentice Hall.

Graham, S., & Freeman, S. (1985). Strategy training and teacher- vs. student-controlled study conditions: Effects on LD students' spelling performance. *Learning Disability Quarterly, 8,* 267–274.

Graham, S., Harris, K.R., MacArthur, C.A., & Schwartz, S. (1991). Writing and writing instruction for students with learning disabilities: Review of a research program. *Learning Disability Quarterly, 14,* 89–114.

Harris, K.R., & Pressley, M. (1991). The nature of cognitive strategy instruction: *Interactive strategy construction. Exceptional Children, 57,* 392–404.

Hendrickson, A. (2001). *World history according to college students: Non campus mentis.* New York: Workman Publishing.

Hughes, C.A., Ruhl, K.L., Schumaker, J.B., & Deshler, D.D. (2002). Effects of instruction in an assignment completion strategy on the homework performance of students with learning disabilities in general education classes. *Learning Disabilities Research and Practice, 17,* 1–18.

Hughes, C.A., & Schumaker, J.B. (1991). Test-taking strategy instruction for adolescents with learning disabilities. *Exceptionality, 2,* 205–221.

King-Sears, M.E., Mercer, C.D., & Sindelar, P. (1992). Toward independence with keyword mnemonics: A strategy for science vocabulary. *Remedial and Special Education, 13*(5), 22–33.

Kurtz B.E., & Borkowski, J.G. (1987). Development of strategic skills in impulsive and reflective children: A longitudinal study of metacognition. *Journal of Experimental and Child Psychology, 43,* 129–148.

Lenz, B.K., & Hughes, C.A. (1990). A word identification strategy for adolescents with learning disabilities. *Journal of Learning Disabilities, 23,* 149–158, 163.

Maccini, P., & Hughes, C.A. (2000). Effects of a problem-solving strategy on the introductory algebra performance of secondary students with learning disabilities. *Learning Disabilities Research and Practice, 15*(1), 10–21.

Mercer, C.D., & Mercer, A.R. (1985). *Teaching students with learning problems.* Columbus, OH: Merrill.

Miller, S.P., & Mercer, C.D. (1993). Using a graduated word problem sequence to promote problem-solving skills. *Learning Disabilities Research and Practice, 8*, 169–174.

Mushinski Fulk, B., & Stormont-Spurgin, M. (1995). Spelling interventions for students with learning disabilities: A review. *The Journal of Special Education, 28*, 488–513.

Nagel, D.R., Schumaker, J.B., & Deshler, D.D. (1986). *The FIRST-letter mnemonic strategy.* Lawrence, KS: Edge Enterprises.

Palincsar, A.S., & Brown, A.L. (1986). Interactive teaching to promote independent learning from text. *Reading Teacher, 39*, 771–777.

Prater, M.A., Chilman, R.J.B., Temple, J., & Miller, S.R. (1991). Self-monitoring of on-task behavior by adolescents with learning disabilities. *Learning Disability Quarterly, 14*, 169.

Pratt-Struthers, J., Struthers, T.B., & Williams, R.L. (1983). The effects of the add-a-word program on spelling accuracy during creative writing. *Education and Treatment of Children, 6*, 277–283.

Schumaker, J.B., Denton, P.H., & Deshler, D.D. (1984). *The paraphrasing strategy.* Lawrence, KS: The University of Kansas.

Schumaker, J.B., & Deshler, D.D. (1984). Setting demand variables: A major factor in program planning for LD adolescents. *Topics in Language Disorders, 4*, 22–44.

Schumaker, J.B., & Deshler, D.D. (1992). Validation of learning strategy interventions for students with LD: Results of a programmatic research effort. In Y.L. Wong (Ed.), *Contemporary intervention research in learning disabilities: An international perspective.* New York: Springer-Verlag.

Schumaker, J.B., & Sheldon, J. (1985). *The sentence writing strategy.* Lawrence, KS: The University of Kansas.

Scruggs, T.E., & Mastropieri, M.A. (1992). Classroom applications of mnemonic instruction: Acquisition, maintenance, and generalization. *Exceptional Children, 58*, 219–229.

Simmons, S.M. (1989). PSRT—A reading comprehension strategy. *Journal of Reading, 32*(5), 419–427.